THE ART OF MARKETING

Mastering the Strategies and Techniques for Business Success

The Art of Marketing: Mastering the Strategies and Techniques for Business Success" provides a comprehensive guide to the world of marketing, covering essential topics such as understanding consumer behavior, crafting marketing strategies, leveraging digital channels, and building long-term customer relationships. This book also delves into the importance of storytelling in marketing, data-driven decision-making, and ethical marketing practices. With a focus on future trends, it prepares readers to adapt and innovate in a rapidly evolving marketing landscape. Whether you're an entrepreneur, marketing professional, or student, this book equips you with the knowledge and skills to excel in the art of marketing

Learning

Chapter 1: Fundamentals of Marketing

Part 1: The Marketing Mix: Product, Price, Place, and Promotion

The marketing mix is the foundation of any successful marketing strategy. It consists of four key elements, known as the 4Ps: Product, Price, Place, and Promotion. Each of these elements plays a vital role in determining the overall success of a marketing campaign. In this part, we will discuss each of the 4Ps and how they work together to create a cohesive marketing strategy.

1. Product: The first element in the marketing mix is the product itself. This refers to the physical goods or services that a company offers to its target customers. A well-designed product meets the needs and wants of its target audience, offering unique features and benefits that set it apart from competitors. To develop a successful product, marketers must conduct thorough market research to identify customer needs, preferences, and pain points.

2. Price: The second element in the marketing mix is price, which refers to the amount a customer is willing to pay for a product or service. Pricing strategy is crucial because it directly affects revenue, profit margins, and the perceived value of a product. Marketers must consider factors such as production costs, market demand, and competitor pricing to set an optimal price that maximizes profitability while remaining attractive to customers.

3. Place: The third element in the marketing mix is place, which refers to the distribution channels used to make a product or service available to customers. Place encompasses both the physical locations where a product is sold, such as retail stores, and the digital channels, such as e-commerce platforms. An effective distribution strategy ensures that products are easily accessible and readily available to target customers, ultimately

increasing the likelihood of a purchase.

4. Promotion: The final element in the marketing mix is promotion, which encompasses all marketing communication activities aimed at raising awareness, generating interest, and driving sales. Promotional strategies can include advertising, public relations, social media marketing, content marketing, and sales promotions. A well-executed promotional campaign helps to create brand recognition, build trust and credibility, and stimulate customer engagement.

In summary, the marketing mix is a crucial framework that helps marketers develop and implement successful marketing strategies. By carefully considering each of the 4Ps—Product, Price, Place, and Promotion—marketers can create a cohesive plan that aligns with their overall business goals and meets the needs of their target customers. Understanding the interplay between these elements is key to creating a strong and effective marketing strategy that drives business success.

Part 2: Market Segmentation and Targeting

Market segmentation and targeting are essential components of any successful marketing strategy. These processes involve dividing a market into distinct groups of consumers with similar needs, preferences, and behaviors, and then focusing marketing efforts on those segments that are most likely to become loyal customers. In this part, we will discuss the importance of market segmentation and targeting, as well as the various methods used to identify and reach target audiences.

1. Importance of Market Segmentation and Targeting: Segmentation and targeting allow businesses to identify their most valuable customers, tailor their marketing messages and product offerings to meet the specific needs of these customers, and allocate resources more efficiently. By targeting specific segments, businesses can achieve higher sales, better customer retention, and improved overall profitability.

2. Criteria for Segmenting Markets: Markets can be segmented based on various factors, including demographic, geographic, psychographic, and behavioral characteristics.

   - Demographic segmentation involves dividing the market based on characteristics such as age, gender, income, education, and family size.

   - Geographic segmentation focuses on the location of customers, such as their country, region, or city.

   - Psychographic segmentation considers the lifestyles, values, attitudes, and interests of consumers.

   - Behavioral segmentation is based on how customers use or interact with a product, their purchasing habits, and their loyalty to the brand.

3. Identifying Target Segments: After segmenting the market,

businesses must evaluate the attractiveness and viability of each segment to determine which are most valuable and worth targeting. Factors to consider when evaluating target segments include segment size, growth potential, profitability, competitive landscape, and alignment with the company's resources and capabilities.

4. Developing Targeting Strategies: Once target segments are identified, businesses must develop strategies to reach these customers effectively. There are four primary targeting strategies to consider:

- Undifferentiated (Mass) Marketing: This approach involves targeting the entire market with a single product or marketing message, aiming to appeal to the largest possible audience.

- Differentiated (Segmented) Marketing: This strategy involves targeting multiple segments with different marketing messages and product offerings tailored to each segment's unique needs.

- Concentrated (Niche) Marketing: This approach focuses on a single, well-defined market segment with a specialized product offering or marketing message, catering to the specific needs of that segment.

- Micromarketing (Individualized Marketing): This highly customized approach involves tailoring marketing messages and products to individual customers or small, highly specific segments.

In conclusion, market segmentation and targeting are critical steps in developing a successful marketing strategy. By understanding the needs and preferences of different consumer groups, businesses can create tailored marketing messages and product offerings that resonate with their target audiences. This focused approach leads to more effective marketing campaigns, increased customer loyalty, and ultimately, improved business performance.

Part 3: Positioning and Differentiation

Positioning and differentiation are crucial aspects of a successful marketing strategy. Positioning refers to the process of creating a unique and advantageous position for a product or brand in the minds of target customers, while differentiation involves establishing distinct differences between a product or brand and its competitors. In this part, we will discuss the importance of positioning and differentiation, as well as the strategies businesses can use to stand out in the market.

1. Importance of Positioning and Differentiation: In today's highly competitive marketplace, businesses must differentiate themselves from competitors to attract and retain customers. Effective positioning and differentiation can lead to increased brand recognition, customer loyalty, and overall market share. By clearly articulating a unique value proposition, companies can set themselves apart from their competitors and create a compelling reason for consumers to choose their products or services.

2. Identifying Unique Selling Proposition (USP): A unique selling proposition (USP) is a statement that articulates the key benefits, features, or qualities of a product or brand that set it apart from its competitors. To identify a USP, businesses should consider the following factors:

   - What are the primary needs and desires of the target market?

   - What unique features or benefits does the product or brand offer that meet these needs and desires?

   - How does the product or brand compare to competitors in terms of quality, value, and customer experience?

   - What emotional or psychological associations can be created to enhance the product or brand's appeal?

3. Positioning Strategies: Businesses can employ various

positioning strategies to create a unique and advantageous position in the minds of target customers. Some common positioning strategies include:

- Attribute or Benefit Positioning: Emphasizing a specific product feature or benefit that sets it apart from competitors.

- Price or Quality Positioning: Focusing on offering either the lowest price or the highest quality in the market.

- Use or Application Positioning: Highlighting unique or innovative uses for a product or service.

- Competitor-Based Positioning: Differentiating a product or brand based on how it compares to competitors, either by outperforming them or occupying a unique niche in the market.

- Emotional or Psychological Positioning: Creating emotional connections with consumers through branding, storytelling, or shared values.

4. Communicating the Positioning: Once a positioning strategy has been developed, it must be effectively communicated to target customers. This can be achieved through various marketing channels, such as advertising, public relations, social media, content marketing, and packaging design. Consistency is key when communicating positioning, as it helps to reinforce the brand's unique position in the minds of consumers and build trust and credibility over time.

In summary, positioning and differentiation are essential elements of a successful marketing strategy. By identifying a unique selling proposition and implementing effective positioning strategies, businesses can create a strong and distinct brand identity that resonates with target customers. This, in turn, can lead to increased brand recognition, customer loyalty, and market share, ultimately driving business success.

Part 4: Building a Strong Brand Identity

A strong brand identity is vital to the success of any marketing strategy. Brand identity refers to the visual, verbal, and emotional elements that define how a company presents itself to the world and distinguishes itself from competitors. In this part, we will discuss the importance of a strong brand identity and provide guidelines for building and maintaining a consistent and compelling brand image.

1. Importance of a Strong Brand Identity: A strong brand identity helps businesses stand out in a crowded marketplace, create a lasting impression on consumers, and foster customer loyalty. It also helps to convey the company's values, mission, and unique selling proposition, while building trust and credibility with target audiences.

2. Elements of Brand Identity: Brand identity consists of several key elements, including:
   - Logo: A unique and recognizable symbol or design that represents the company and is easily identifiable by consumers.
   - Color Palette: A consistent set of colors used across all marketing materials and touchpoints to create a cohesive brand image.
   - Typography: The selection and consistent use of fonts to convey the brand's personality and style.
   - Imagery: Visual elements such as photographs, illustrations, and graphics used to convey the brand's message and create an emotional connection with consumers.
   - Tone of Voice: The consistent verbal style and personality used in all written and spoken communications.

3. Developing a Brand Identity: To create a strong brand identity,

businesses should follow these steps:

- Define the Brand's Core Values: Identify the fundamental beliefs and principles that guide the company and underpin its purpose.

- Determine the Target Audience: Clearly define the ideal customer profile, considering demographic, psychographic, and behavioral characteristics.

- Craft a Unique Selling Proposition (USP): Articulate the key features or benefits that differentiate the brand from competitors and make it appealing to the target audience.

- Develop a Brand Personality: Determine the characteristics and traits that the brand should embody, such as friendly, authoritative, or innovative.

- Create a Visual Identity: Design a logo, choose a color palette, and select typography and imagery that reflect the brand's personality and values.

4. Maintaining Brand Consistency: To build a strong brand identity, businesses must maintain consistency across all marketing channels and touchpoints. This includes using the same logo, color palette, typography, imagery, and tone of voice in all communications and ensuring that the brand's core values and USP are consistently communicated. Consistency helps to reinforce the brand's identity in the minds of consumers, building trust and credibility over time.

In conclusion, building a strong brand identity is a crucial aspect of a successful marketing strategy. By defining the brand's core values, target audience, and unique selling proposition, and developing a consistent visual and verbal identity, businesses can create a lasting impression on consumers and differentiate themselves from competitors. A strong brand identity fosters customer loyalty, trust, and credibility, ultimately driving business success.

Chapter 2: Understanding Consumer Behavior

Part 1: The Consumer Decision-Making Process

Understanding consumer behavior is essential for creating effective marketing strategies. The consumer decision-making process involves the series of steps that consumers go through when deciding to purchase a product or service. In this part, we will discuss the stages of the consumer decision-making process and explore the factors that influence consumer choices.

1. Stages of the Consumer Decision-Making Process: The consumer decision-making process typically consists of five stages:

- Problem Recognition: The consumer realizes that they have an unmet need or desire, prompting them to search for a solution.

- Information Search: The consumer gathers information about potential products or services that can fulfill their need or desire. This can involve searching online, seeking recommendations from friends, or visiting stores.

- Evaluation of Alternatives: The consumer compares the different products or services available, considering factors such as price, quality, features, and brand reputation.

- Purchase Decision: The consumer selects the product or service that best meets their needs and desires and proceeds with the purchase.

- Post-Purchase Behavior: After the purchase, the consumer evaluates the product or service based on their satisfaction with its performance, ultimately influencing future purchase decisions and brand loyalty.

2. Factors Influencing Consumer Behavior: A variety of factors can

influence the consumer decision-making process, including:

- Personal Factors: These include individual characteristics such as age, gender, personality, lifestyle, and income.

- Psychological Factors: These encompass cognitive processes such as motivation, perception, learning, and attitudes, which shape how consumers interpret and respond to marketing messages.

- Social Factors: These involve the influence of family, friends, social groups, and cultural norms on consumer choices.

- Situational Factors: These refer to specific circumstances or contexts that can impact consumer behavior, such as time constraints, mood, or physical environment.

3. Implications for Marketing: Understanding the consumer decision-making process and the factors that influence it allows marketers to develop more effective marketing strategies. By identifying the needs and desires of their target audience and the factors that influence their choices, marketers can create tailored marketing messages and product offerings that resonate with consumers. Additionally, marketers can use this understanding to design marketing campaigns that guide consumers through each stage of the decision-making process, ultimately driving sales and fostering brand loyalty.

In summary, the consumer decision-making process is a crucial aspect of understanding consumer behavior. By recognizing the stages of the process and the factors that influence consumer choices, marketers can develop targeted marketing strategies that resonate with their audience and drive business success. Gaining insight into the consumer decision-making process allows businesses to create more compelling marketing messages, tailor product offerings to meet consumer needs, and ultimately, cultivate lasting customer relationships.

Part 2: Psychological Factors Influencing Consumer Choices

Psychological factors play a significant role in shaping consumer choices and behavior. These factors encompass cognitive processes and mental states that affect how consumers perceive, interpret, and respond to marketing stimuli. In this part, we will discuss the key psychological factors influencing consumer choices and their implications for marketing strategies.

1. Motivation: Motivation refers to the internal drive or desire that prompts consumers to take action, such as purchasing a product or service. Consumers have various needs and desires that motivate their behavior, ranging from basic physiological needs (e.g., hunger) to higher-level psychological needs (e.g., self-esteem). Marketers can tap into these motivational drivers by creating marketing messages and product offerings that address consumers' specific needs and desires.

2. Perception: Perception is the process through which consumers interpret and make sense of the information they receive from the world around them. Factors such as selective attention, selective distortion, and selective retention can influence how consumers perceive marketing messages and form opinions about products or brands. To ensure that their marketing messages are effectively perceived, marketers should create clear, concise, and compelling content that stands out from the competition and aligns with consumers' beliefs and expectations.

3. Learning: Learning refers to the process through which consumers acquire knowledge, skills, and attitudes based on their experiences and exposure to marketing stimuli. Learning can occur through direct experience, observation, or conditioning, and can shape consumers' preferences, habits, and brand loyalty. Marketers can facilitate learning by providing consumers with engaging, informative, and memorable experiences, as well as

leveraging repetition and reinforcement to strengthen brand associations.

4. Memory: Memory involves the storage and retrieval of information, which can influence consumers' decision-making processes and future behavior. Factors such as the primacy and recency effects, as well as the level of processing, can impact how easily consumers remember marketing messages and product information. To enhance memory retention, marketers should create memorable marketing messages and product experiences that are easily processed and encoded into long-term memory.

5. Attitudes: Attitudes are the mental evaluations, feelings, and beliefs that consumers hold towards products, brands, or marketing messages. Attitudes are influenced by cognitive, affective, and behavioral components and can play a significant role in shaping consumer preferences and purchase decisions. Marketers can influence consumer attitudes by creating persuasive marketing messages, appealing to consumers' emotions, and providing positive product experiences.

In conclusion, understanding the psychological factors that influence consumer choices is crucial for creating effective marketing strategies. By considering the role of motivation, perception, learning, memory, and attitudes, marketers can develop targeted marketing messages and product offerings that resonate with consumers and drive desired behaviors. By tapping into these psychological factors, marketers can enhance the effectiveness of their marketing campaigns, foster strong consumer-brand relationships, and ultimately, drive business success.

Part 3: Social and Cultural Influences on Consumer Behavior

Social and cultural factors have a significant impact on consumer behavior, shaping the choices consumers make and the preferences they develop. These influences come from various sources, including family, friends, social groups, and cultural norms. In this part, we will discuss the key social and cultural influences on consumer behavior and their implications for marketing strategies.

1. Family and Friends: Family and friends can influence consumer behavior through their recommendations, opinions, and shared experiences. Consumers often seek advice from their close social circle when making purchase decisions, making word-of-mouth marketing and referrals a powerful tool for businesses. Marketers can leverage the influence of family and friends by encouraging satisfied customers to share their experiences and recommend products or services to others.

2. Social Groups and Reference Groups: Social groups, such as peer groups, professional associations, and clubs, can also shape consumer behavior by establishing group norms, values, and expectations. Reference groups, which are groups that individuals aspire to or identify with, can influence consumers' product choices and brand preferences. To appeal to specific social and reference groups, marketers can create targeted marketing messages that resonate with these groups' values and aspirations, as well as collaborate with influential group members or ambassadors.

3. Social Class: Social class, defined by factors such as income, education, and occupation, can influence consumers' purchasing power, product preferences, and brand loyalty. Different social classes often have distinct consumption patterns, preferences, and values, which can impact their response to marketing

messages and product offerings. Marketers can tailor their marketing strategies to appeal to specific social classes by understanding and addressing their unique needs, desires, and preferences.

4. Culture and Subculture: Culture refers to the shared beliefs, values, customs, and behaviors of a particular group or society, while subculture encompasses the distinct beliefs and behaviors of smaller groups within a larger culture. Cultural and subcultural factors can significantly influence consumers' attitudes, preferences, and consumption patterns. To cater to the diverse cultural and subcultural groups, marketers can create culturally sensitive marketing messages, offer products and services that align with specific cultural values, and adapt their marketing strategies to accommodate cultural nuances and preferences.

5. Opinion Leaders and Influencers: Opinion leaders and influencers are individuals who have a significant impact on the opinions and behaviors of others due to their perceived expertise, charisma, or social status. These individuals can shape consumer behavior by endorsing products, sharing their experiences, or offering advice. Marketers can collaborate with opinion leaders and influencers to promote their products or services, leveraging their credibility and reach to influence consumer choices.

In conclusion, understanding the social and cultural influences on consumer behavior is crucial for creating effective marketing strategies. By considering the impact of family and friends, social and reference groups, social class, culture and subculture, and opinion leaders and influencers, marketers can develop targeted marketing messages and product offerings that resonate with their audience and drive desired behaviors. By tapping into these social and cultural factors, marketers can enhance the effectiveness of their marketing campaigns, foster strong consumer-brand relationships, and ultimately, drive business success.

Part 4: Leveraging Consumer Insights for Effective Marketing

Consumer insights, or the deep understanding of consumers' needs, preferences, and motivations, are invaluable for developing effective marketing strategies. By leveraging these insights, marketers can create targeted marketing messages, product offerings, and customer experiences that resonate with their audience and drive desired behaviors. In this part, we will discuss how to leverage consumer insights for effective marketing.

1. Conducting Market Research: Market research is essential for gaining consumer insights and understanding the target audience's needs, preferences, and motivations. Various research methods, such as surveys, interviews, focus groups, and observational studies, can be employed to gather data on consumer behavior. Additionally, marketers can analyze secondary data, such as industry reports and social media trends, to gain insights into consumer preferences and emerging market trends.

2. Developing Customer Personas: Customer personas are fictional representations of the target audience, created based on consumer insights gathered from market research. By developing detailed customer personas, marketers can gain a deeper understanding of their audience's needs, preferences, and motivations, allowing them to create tailored marketing messages and product offerings that resonate with their audience.

3. Creating Segmentation Strategies: Segmentation involves dividing the target audience into smaller, homogenous groups based on shared characteristics, such as demographics, psychographics, or behavior. By leveraging consumer insights to create effective segmentation strategies, marketers can develop targeted marketing campaigns and product offerings that cater to the unique needs and preferences of each segment, ultimately

driving engagement and sales.

4. Personalizing Marketing Messages: Personalization involves tailoring marketing messages and customer experiences to meet the individual needs and preferences of each consumer. By leveraging consumer insights to personalize marketing messages, marketers can create more relevant and engaging content that resonates with their audience, ultimately increasing the likelihood of conversion and fostering customer loyalty.

5. Enhancing Product Development: Consumer insights can also inform product development by identifying unmet needs, preferences, and pain points within the target market. By incorporating these insights into product design and development, marketers can create products that better meet the needs of their audience, differentiate themselves from competitors, and ultimately, drive sales.

6. Monitoring and Adapting: Consumer preferences and behaviors are constantly evolving, making it essential for marketers to continually monitor and adapt their marketing strategies based on emerging consumer insights. By staying abreast of changes in consumer behavior and market trends, marketers can adjust their marketing messages, product offerings, and customer experiences to remain relevant and effective.

In conclusion, leveraging consumer insights is crucial for developing effective marketing strategies that resonate with the target audience and drive desired behaviors. By conducting market research, developing customer personas, creating segmentation strategies, personalizing marketing messages, enhancing product development, and monitoring and adapting to changes in consumer behavior, marketers can create compelling marketing campaigns that foster strong consumer-brand relationships and ultimately, drive business success.

Chapter 3: Crafting a Compelling Marketing Strategy

Part 1: Setting Clear Marketing Objectives

A compelling marketing strategy begins with setting clear marketing objectives that align with the overall business goals. These objectives serve as a roadmap for the marketing activities and help to measure the effectiveness of the strategy. In this part, we will discuss the importance of setting clear marketing objectives and provide guidance on how to establish them.

1. Importance of Marketing Objectives: Marketing objectives are essential for several reasons:

- Direction: Clear objectives provide direction for marketing activities, ensuring that resources are allocated effectively and marketing efforts are focused on achieving specific outcomes.

- Alignment: Objectives ensure that marketing activities align with the overall business goals, supporting the broader strategic vision of the company.

- Measurement: By establishing measurable objectives, marketers can track the progress and success of their marketing efforts, making it easier to identify areas for improvement and adjust the strategy accordingly.

2. Characteristics of Effective Marketing Objectives: To be effective, marketing objectives should be:

- Specific: Objectives should be precise and clearly defined, providing a clear understanding of what the marketing efforts aim to achieve.

- Measurable: Objectives should be quantifiable, enabling marketers to track progress and assess the effectiveness of the strategy.

- Achievable: Objectives should be realistic and attainable, considering the available resources, market conditions, and competition.

- Relevant: Objectives should align with the overall business goals and be relevant to the target audience and market.

- Time-bound: Objectives should have a specific timeline, creating a sense of urgency and enabling marketers to evaluate the success of the strategy within a set timeframe.

3. Establishing Marketing Objectives: To set effective marketing objectives, consider the following steps:

- Review the overall business goals and identify how marketing can support these objectives. This may involve increasing brand awareness, driving sales, or improving customer retention.

- Conduct market research to gain insights into the target audience, competition, and market trends. This information will help to inform the marketing objectives and ensure they are relevant and achievable.

- Identify specific, measurable goals for each marketing objective. These may include metrics such as website traffic, social media engagement, lead generation, or sales revenue.

- Establish a timeline for achieving the objectives, setting short-term and long-term goals that align with the overall business strategy.

- Communicate the marketing objectives to the marketing team and relevant stakeholders, ensuring that everyone is aligned and working towards the same goals.

In summary, setting clear marketing objectives is an essential first step in crafting a compelling marketing strategy. By establishing specific, measurable, achievable, relevant, and time-bound objectives, marketers can create a focused and effective marketing plan that aligns with the overall business goals, drives desired outcomes, and fosters long-term success.

Part 2: Analyzing Market Opportunities and Threats

A thorough analysis of market opportunities and threats is crucial for crafting a successful marketing strategy. By understanding the external factors that can positively or negatively impact the business, marketers can make informed decisions and tailor their marketing efforts to capitalize on opportunities and mitigate risks. In this part, we will discuss the importance of analyzing market opportunities and threats and provide guidance on how to conduct this analysis.

1. Importance of Market Analysis: Conducting a comprehensive market analysis is essential for several reasons:

- Identifying Opportunities: By analyzing the market, marketers can uncover untapped opportunities that can drive business growth, such as emerging trends, market gaps, or new target segments.

- Recognizing Threats: Market analysis also helps to identify potential risks and challenges, such as increased competition, changing consumer preferences, or regulatory changes, enabling businesses to prepare and adapt accordingly.

- Guiding Strategy: A thorough market analysis informs marketing strategy, helping businesses to prioritize their efforts, allocate resources effectively, and tailor their marketing messages and product offerings to the market's needs and preferences.

2. Conducting Market Analysis: To analyze market opportunities and threats, consider the following steps:

- Industry Overview: Begin by assessing the overall industry landscape, including market size, growth trends, key players, and industry-specific factors that can impact the business.

- Competitor Analysis: Analyze the competition, examining their market share, product offerings, marketing strategies, strengths, and weaknesses. Identify potential competitive advantages that can be leveraged to differentiate the business.

- Consumer Analysis: Study the target audience, exploring their needs, preferences, pain points, and motivations. Identify any unmet needs or market gaps that the business can address.

- Market Trends: Examine current and emerging market trends that can create opportunities or threats, such as technological advancements, shifts in consumer behavior, or changes in the economic or regulatory environment.

3. Utilizing Market Analysis in Marketing Strategy:

- Capitalize on Opportunities: Use the insights gained from market analysis to identify and prioritize marketing efforts that exploit market opportunities. This may involve targeting new market segments, addressing unmet needs, or adapting product offerings to capitalize on emerging trends.

- Mitigate Threats: Develop strategies to address identified threats, such as enhancing the product offering, improving marketing messages, or adjusting pricing strategies to remain competitive.

- Differentiate from Competitors: Leverage the competitor analysis to differentiate the business from its rivals, highlighting unique selling points, targeting underserved market segments, or positioning the brand to appeal to specific consumer preferences.

In conclusion, analyzing market opportunities and threats is a critical step in crafting a compelling marketing strategy. By conducting a thorough market analysis, marketers can identify and prioritize opportunities, recognize and address potential risks, and differentiate their business from the competition. This process ultimately leads to the development of a marketing strategy that is tailored to the market's needs and preferences, enhancing the business's chances of success.

Part 3: Assessing Competitive Advantage

A competitive advantage is a unique feature or characteristic that allows a business to outperform its competitors. Identifying and leveraging these advantages is crucial for developing an effective marketing strategy that differentiates the business in the marketplace and attracts customers. In this part, we will discuss the importance of assessing competitive advantage and provide guidance on how to identify and leverage these advantages in marketing strategy.

1. Importance of Competitive Advantage: A competitive advantage is essential for several reasons:

- Differentiation: A competitive advantage helps a business to stand out from its competitors by offering unique value to customers.

- Customer Attraction: By highlighting a competitive advantage, businesses can attract customers who are specifically seeking the unique benefits that the company offers.

- Profitability: A competitive advantage can drive profitability by enabling a business to charge a premium for its unique offering or by attracting a larger market share.

- Market Position: A strong competitive advantage can solidify a business's position in the market and create a barrier to entry for potential competitors.

2. Identifying Competitive Advantages: To identify competitive advantages, consider the following factors:

- Product or Service Features: Assess the unique attributes of the product or service offering, such as quality, functionality, design, or innovation.

- Brand Reputation: Evaluate the brand's reputation, including brand awareness, customer loyalty, and perceived quality or value.

- Customer Service: Analyze the level of customer service provided, such as responsiveness, personalization, or after-sales support.

- Distribution Channels: Examine the efficiency and reach of the distribution channels, including online presence, retail partnerships, or direct sales capabilities.

- Pricing Strategy: Assess the pricing strategy and whether it offers a unique advantage, such as a cost leadership or premium pricing approach.

- Organizational Capabilities: Identify any unique organizational capabilities, such as operational efficiency, technological expertise, or a skilled workforce.

3. Leveraging Competitive Advantages in Marketing Strategy:

- Communicate the Advantage: Highlight the competitive advantage in marketing messages, showcasing the unique value proposition that the business offers to customers.

- Target the Right Audience: Identify and target customer segments that value the competitive advantage, focusing marketing efforts on attracting customers who are most likely to appreciate the unique offering.

- Enhance the Advantage: Continuously improve and innovate to strengthen the competitive advantage, ensuring that the business remains ahead of its competitors.

- Monitor the Competition: Keep a close eye on competitors, staying informed of any changes in their offerings or strategies that may impact the competitive advantage.

In conclusion, assessing competitive advantage is a crucial step in crafting a compelling marketing strategy. By identifying and leveraging the unique advantages that a business possesses, marketers can create a differentiated marketing strategy that attracts customers and drives profitability. This process ultimately leads to a stronger market position and long-term business success.

Part 4: Developing a Cohesive Marketing Action Plan

Once the marketing objectives, market opportunities, and competitive advantages have been identified, the next step is to develop a cohesive marketing action plan. This plan outlines the specific marketing tactics and activities that will be implemented to achieve the marketing objectives, capitalize on market opportunities, and leverage competitive advantages. In this part, we will discuss the importance of developing a cohesive marketing action plan and provide guidance on how to create one.

1. Importance of a Marketing Action Plan: A marketing action plan is essential for several reasons:

   - Focus: The plan provides a clear focus for marketing efforts, ensuring that resources are allocated effectively and activities are targeted towards achieving the marketing objectives.

   - Coordination: A cohesive action plan helps to coordinate marketing activities across different channels, teams, and stakeholders, ensuring a consistent and unified marketing message.

   - Measurement: The plan establishes a framework for measuring the success of marketing efforts, enabling marketers to track progress, identify areas for improvement, and adjust the strategy as needed.

2. Components of a Marketing Action Plan: A comprehensive marketing action plan should include the following components:

   - Marketing Objectives: Clearly state the specific, measurable, achievable, relevant, and time-bound marketing objectives that the plan aims to achieve.

   - Target Audience: Define the target audience segments that the marketing efforts will be focused on, including demographics, psychographics, and behavioral characteristics.

- Marketing Channels: Identify the marketing channels that will be used to reach the target audience, such as digital channels (social media, email, content marketing), traditional channels (print, radio, television), or events and experiential marketing.

- Marketing Tactics: Outline the specific marketing tactics that will be implemented within each channel, such as content creation, advertising campaigns, or promotional activities.

- Timeline: Establish a timeline for implementing the marketing activities, specifying the start and end dates for each tactic or campaign.

- Budget: Allocate a budget for each marketing activity, ensuring that resources are distributed effectively and aligned with the marketing objectives.

- Key Performance Indicators (KPIs): Define the KPIs that will be used to measure the success of the marketing efforts, such as website traffic, conversion rates, or sales revenue.

3. Developing a Cohesive Marketing Action Plan: To create a cohesive marketing action plan, consider the following steps:

- Review the marketing objectives, market analysis, and competitive advantages, ensuring that the marketing activities are aligned with these insights.

- Brainstorm marketing tactics and activities that will effectively achieve the marketing objectives, capitalize on market opportunities, and leverage competitive advantages.

- Prioritize marketing activities based on their potential impact, feasibility, and alignment with the marketing objectives and target audience preferences.

- Create a detailed plan, outlining the specific marketing tactics, channels, timeline, budget, and KPIs for each activity.

- Communicate the marketing action plan to the marketing team and relevant stakeholders, ensuring that everyone is aligned and working towards the same goals.

In conclusion, developing a cohesive marketing action plan is a critical step in crafting a compelling marketing strategy. By outlining the specific marketing tactics, channels, timeline, budget, and KPIs that will be implemented to achieve the marketing objectives, marketers can create a focused and effective marketing plan that drives desired outcomes and fosters long-term success.

Chapter 4: The Power of Storytelling in Marketing

Part 1: The Science and Art of Storytelling

Storytelling has been an integral part of human communication for thousands of years. In marketing, storytelling is a powerful tool for connecting with audiences and conveying messages in a memorable, engaging, and emotionally impactful way. In this part, we will explore the science and art of storytelling, discussing its importance in marketing and providing guidance on how to incorporate storytelling into marketing efforts.

1. Importance of Storytelling in Marketing: Storytelling is crucial in marketing for several reasons:

- Emotional Connection: Stories evoke emotions, making it easier for audiences to connect with a brand, product, or message on a deeper level.

- Memorability: Stories are more memorable than facts or statistics, increasing the likelihood that audiences will recall the marketing message.

- Persuasion: Stories can be persuasive, helping to influence audiences and shape their perceptions, attitudes, or behaviors.

- Differentiation: A compelling story can set a brand apart from its competitors, highlighting its unique value proposition and fostering brand loyalty.

2. The Science of Storytelling: Several psychological factors contribute to the power of storytelling:

- Neurological Processing: Stories activate multiple areas of the brain, including those responsible for sensory processing, emotion, and memory, making them more engaging and memorable.

- Empathy: When listening to a story, people tend to empathize with the characters, experiencing their emotions and becoming more invested in the narrative.

- Cognitive Ease: Stories follow a familiar structure and often use relatable characters and situations, making them easy for audiences to understand and process.

3. The Art of Storytelling: To incorporate storytelling into marketing efforts, consider the following elements:

- Structure: A classic story structure includes a beginning (setting the scene and introducing characters), a middle (presenting challenges or conflicts), and an end (resolving the challenges and offering a takeaway). This structure can be adapted to fit various marketing formats, such as advertisements, blog posts, or case studies.

- Characters: Develop relatable and compelling characters, such as customers, employees, or the brand itself, to engage audiences and evoke empathy.

- Conflict: Introduce a conflict or challenge that the characters must overcome, such as a problem the target audience faces, which the product or service can help solve.

- Resolution: Offer a resolution to the conflict, showcasing how the product or service can positively impact the characters or the target audience.

- Takeaway: Conclude the story with a clear takeaway, such as a call to action, a key message, or a lesson learned.

In summary, the power of storytelling lies in its ability to evoke emotions, create memorable experiences, and influence audience perceptions. By understanding the science and art of storytelling, marketers can incorporate stories into their marketing efforts to connect with audiences, convey messages effectively, and differentiate their brand from competitors.

Part 2: Crafting Your Brand's Story

Creating a compelling brand story is crucial for establishing an emotional connection with your target audience, differentiating your brand from competitors, and conveying your brand's unique value proposition. In this part, we will discuss the process of crafting your brand's story and provide guidance on how to effectively incorporate it into your marketing efforts.

1. Defining Your Brand's Core Values: The foundation of your brand's story lies in its core values, which are the principles and beliefs that guide your company's actions and decision-making. Start by identifying and articulating your brand's core values, such as innovation, sustainability, or customer-centricity. These values should be authentic, meaningful, and aligned with your brand's mission and vision.

2. Developing Your Brand's Narrative: With your core values in place, you can begin to develop your brand's narrative. This narrative should be rooted in your values and communicate what sets your brand apart from its competitors. Consider the following elements when crafting your brand's narrative:

- Origin Story: Share the story of how your company was founded, what inspired its creation, and how it has evolved over time.

- Purpose: Clearly articulate your brand's purpose, or the reason it exists beyond making a profit. This purpose should be meaningful, inspiring, and aligned with your core values.

- Customer Stories: Showcase real-life customer stories that demonstrate how your brand has positively impacted their lives or solved their problems.

- Future Vision: Paint a picture of your brand's future vision, describing how it aims to continue making a difference and creating value for its customers and stakeholders.

3. Incorporating Your Brand's Story into Marketing Efforts: Once you've crafted your brand's story, it's essential to incorporate it into your marketing efforts. Here are some tips for doing so effectively:

- Consistency: Ensure that your brand's story is consistently communicated across all marketing channels and touchpoints, such as your website, social media, and advertising campaigns.

- Storytelling Formats: Utilize various storytelling formats, such as written content, videos, podcasts, or events, to convey your brand's story in a way that resonates with your target audience.

- Employee Advocacy: Encourage employees to share your brand's story with their networks, fostering a sense of pride and ownership in the company's values and narrative.

- Brand Collateral: Incorporate your brand's story into its visual identity, including logo design, packaging, and promotional materials, to create a cohesive brand experience.

4. Measuring the Impact of Your Brand's Story: To assess the effectiveness of your brand's story, establish key performance indicators (KPIs) that align with your marketing objectives, such as brand awareness, engagement, or customer loyalty. Track these KPIs over time to gauge the impact of your storytelling efforts and identify areas for improvement.

In conclusion, crafting your brand's story is a critical component of successful marketing efforts. By defining your brand's core values, developing a compelling narrative, incorporating the story into your marketing efforts, and measuring its impact, you can foster emotional connections with your audience, differentiate your brand from competitors, and create lasting brand loyalty.

Part 3: Integrating Storytelling in Marketing Communications

Effectively integrating storytelling into marketing communications helps create more engaging, memorable, and emotionally resonant content. In this part, we will discuss various marketing communication channels and provide guidance on how to incorporate storytelling into each channel to maximize its impact.

1. Content Marketing: Content marketing provides an excellent opportunity to share your brand's story through blog posts, articles, whitepapers, or e-books. Create content that weaves your brand's narrative into topics that interest your target audience, showcasing your expertise and providing valuable insights while reinforcing your brand's core values and purpose.

2. Social Media Marketing: Social media platforms offer a unique way to connect with your audience on a personal level. Share stories about your brand, customers, employees, or industry that resonate with your followers. Use a mix of formats, such as images, videos, and text, to create engaging content that encourages sharing and interaction.

3. Email Marketing: Email campaigns can be an effective channel for sharing stories with your subscribers. Craft compelling email content that incorporates storytelling elements, such as customer success stories, behind-the-scenes looks at your company, or narratives that showcase your brand's values and purpose.

4. Advertising: Integrating storytelling into advertising campaigns can make them more memorable and persuasive. Create ads that tell a story, whether it's through a single image, a series of images, or a video. Focus on conveying your brand's unique value proposition and connecting with your audience emotionally.

5. Public Relations: Leverage storytelling in your public relations efforts by crafting press releases, media pitches, and articles that share compelling stories about your brand, products, or services. Highlight your company's achievements, innovations, or social impact, and position your brand as an industry leader or change-maker.

6. Events and Experiential Marketing: In-person and virtual events provide an opportunity to bring your brand's story to life through immersive experiences. Create event themes, presentations, or activities that showcase your brand's narrative and connect with attendees on an emotional level.

7. Video Marketing: Video is a powerful medium for storytelling, as it combines visuals, audio, and narrative to create a captivating experience. Develop videos that share your brand's story or highlight customer experiences, incorporating elements such as interviews, testimonials, or animated explainer videos.

To effectively integrate storytelling into marketing communications, keep the following best practices in mind:

- Maintain consistency: Ensure that your brand's story and messaging remain consistent across all marketing channels and touchpoints.
- Keep it authentic: Share genuine stories that reflect your brand's values and purpose, avoiding exaggerated or misleading narratives.
- Adapt to the medium: Tailor your storytelling approach to suit the specific characteristics and constraints of each marketing channel.
- Engage your audience: Encourage audience interaction and feedback by asking questions, inviting user-generated content, or

creating opportunities for conversation.

In conclusion, integrating storytelling into marketing communications can enhance the impact of your marketing efforts by creating more engaging, memorable, and emotionally resonant content. By incorporating storytelling across various marketing channels and adapting your approach to suit each medium, you can effectively convey your brand's unique value proposition and connect with your target audience on a deeper level.

Part 4: Measuring the Impact of Storytelling on Marketing Success

To evaluate the effectiveness of your storytelling efforts and optimize your marketing strategies, it's crucial to measure the impact of storytelling on marketing success. In this part, we will discuss the key performance indicators (KPIs) you can track to assess the success of your storytelling campaigns and identify areas for improvement.

1. Brand Awareness: Storytelling can help increase brand awareness, making your brand more recognizable and top-of-mind for consumers. KPIs to track for brand awareness include:

- Reach: The number of people exposed to your storytelling content across various channels, such as website visitors, social media impressions, or email opens.

- Brand Mentions: The number of times your brand is mentioned in online conversations, media coverage, or user-generated content.

- Brand Recall: The percentage of your target audience who can recall your brand when prompted, often measured through surveys or interviews.

2. Audience Engagement: Engaging content encourages interaction and fosters a connection between your brand and its audience. KPIs to measure audience engagement include:

- Likes, Shares, and Comments: Track the number of likes, shares, and comments your storytelling content receives on social media platforms.

- Time Spent on Content: Analyze the average time users spend consuming your storytelling content, such as reading blog posts or watching videos.

- Content Downloads: Monitor the number of downloads for

content pieces like e-books, whitepapers, or case studies that incorporate storytelling elements.

3. Conversion Rates: Effective storytelling can drive users to take desired actions, such as making a purchase, signing up for a newsletter, or contacting your sales team. KPIs to track conversion rates include:

- Conversion Rate: The percentage of users who complete a desired action after being exposed to your storytelling content.

- Cost per Conversion: The average amount spent on marketing efforts to achieve one conversion, helping you assess the cost-effectiveness of your storytelling campaigns.

4. Customer Loyalty and Retention: Storytelling can help foster customer loyalty and improve retention rates by creating an emotional connection with your brand. KPIs to measure customer loyalty and retention include:

- Repeat Purchases: Track the number of customers who make multiple purchases or engage with your brand consistently over time.

- Net Promoter Score (NPS): Measure your customers' willingness to recommend your brand to others, which can indicate their level of satisfaction and loyalty.

- Customer Lifetime Value (CLV): Calculate the projected revenue a customer will generate throughout their relationship with your brand, taking into account factors like purchase frequency and average order value.

To effectively measure the impact of storytelling on marketing success, consider the following tips:

- Set clear objectives: Establish specific, measurable, achievable, relevant, and time-bound (SMART) objectives for your storytelling campaigns, and select the KPIs that align with these objectives.

- Use analytics tools: Utilize various analytics tools to track your KPIs, such as Google Analytics for website metrics, social media analytics platforms for engagement metrics, or customer relationship management (CRM) systems for customer loyalty and retention data.

- Conduct regular assessments: Periodically assess your storytelling efforts' performance, comparing results to your objectives and industry benchmarks to identify areas for improvement and optimize your strategies.

- Test and iterate: Conduct A/B testing or other experimentation methods to determine the most effective storytelling approaches, and continuously refine your marketing tactics based on data-driven insights.

In conclusion, measuring the impact of storytelling on marketing success is crucial for optimizing your marketing strategies and maximizing results. By tracking relevant KPIs, setting clear objectives, using analytics tools, and conducting regular assessments, you can effectively evaluate the effectiveness of your marketing campaign.

Chapter 5: Digital Marketing Mastery

Part 1: Search Engine Optimization and Marketing

In today's digital landscape, a solid online presence is essential for any brand looking to thrive. Search engine optimization (SEO) and search engine marketing (SEM) are two critical components of digital marketing that can help your brand attract, engage, and convert online users. In this part, we will explore the fundamentals of SEO and SEM, along with effective strategies to improve your brand's visibility in search engine results.

1. Search Engine Optimization (SEO): SEO involves optimizing your website and content to rank higher in organic search engine results, driving more traffic and visibility for your brand. Key aspects of SEO include:

- Keyword Research: Identify relevant, high-volume keywords that your target audience is searching for and incorporate them into your website's content, metadata, and URLs.

- On-page Optimization: Improve your website's structure, design, and user experience to create a seamless and enjoyable experience for visitors. Focus on elements such as site speed, mobile-friendliness, and easy navigation.

- Content Creation: Develop high-quality, valuable, and engaging content that addresses your target audience's needs and interests. Use various content formats, such as blog posts, articles, videos, and infographics, to cater to different user preferences.

- Off-page Optimization: Build a strong backlink profile by earning high-quality, relevant backlinks from authoritative websites. Leverage strategies like guest blogging, influencer outreach, and social media sharing to increase your site's credibility and authority in the eyes of search engines.

2. Search Engine Marketing (SEM): SEM encompasses paid advertising efforts aimed at increasing your website's visibility in search engine results pages (SERPs). The most common form of SEM is pay-per-click (PPC) advertising, where advertisers bid on keywords to display their ads in search results. Key aspects of SEM include:

- Keyword Strategy: Select relevant, high-converting keywords for your ad campaigns, taking into account factors like search volume, competition, and cost-per-click (CPC).

- Ad Creation: Craft compelling ad copy and visuals that resonate with your target audience and encourage them to click on your ad. Utilize ad extensions, such as sitelinks or callouts, to provide additional information and improve click-through rates (CTRs).

- Landing Page Optimization: Design and optimize landing pages that align with your ad messaging and provide a seamless experience for users. Focus on clear calls-to-action (CTAs), engaging visuals, and persuasive copy that drives conversions.

- Campaign Management: Regularly monitor and optimize your ad campaigns, adjusting bids, targeting, and ad creatives to maximize performance and return on investment (ROI).

To effectively leverage SEO and SEM in your digital marketing strategy, consider the following tips:

- Integrate SEO and SEM Efforts: Coordinate your SEO and SEM strategies to ensure consistent messaging and targeting across both organic and paid search efforts. Use insights from one channel to inform the other, such as leveraging high-performing organic keywords in your PPC campaigns.

- Monitor and Analyze Performance: Use analytics tools like Google Analytics and Google Ads to track your SEO and

SEM performance, monitoring key metrics such as traffic, CTR, conversion rate, and ROI. Use these insights to inform data-driven optimizations and improvements.

- Stay Up-to-Date on Industry Trends: Search engine algorithms and best practices are constantly evolving. Stay informed about the latest developments in the SEO and SEM landscape to ensure your strategies remain effective and compliant with search engine guidelines.

- Be Patient and Persistent: SEO and SEM efforts often require time to produce significant results. Be patient and persistent in implementing and refining your strategies, continuously learning and adapting to achieve long-term success.

In conclusion, mastering SEO and SEM is crucial for any brand looking to excel.

Part 2: Social Media Marketing and Advertising

In the digital age, social media has become a powerful platform for brands to engage with their target audience, build brand awareness, and drive sales. Social media marketing and advertising involve leveraging various social platforms to promote your brand, products, or services. In this part, we will discuss the key elements of successful social media marketing and advertising strategies and provide actionable tips for maximizing your brand's social media presence.

1. Platform Selection: Choose the social media platforms that align with your brand's target audience, goals, and resources. Consider factors such as user demographics, platform features, and content formats when making your selection. Popular platforms include Facebook, Instagram, Twitter, LinkedIn, Pinterest, and TikTok.

2. Content Strategy: Develop a content strategy that caters to your target audience's interests, needs, and preferences. Create a mix of content types, such as images, videos, text, and stories, and focus on providing value, entertainment, and engagement. Plan your content in advance with a social media content calendar.

3. Brand Voice and Visual Identity: Maintain a consistent brand voice and visual identity across all social media platforms. This consistency will help reinforce your brand's personality and make it more recognizable to your audience. Adapt your messaging and visuals to suit the unique characteristics of each platform.

4. Engagement and Community Building: Foster genuine connections with your audience by actively engaging with them through likes, comments, shares, and direct messages. Respond promptly to questions, feedback, and concerns, and encourage user-generated content and conversations to create a sense of

community around your brand.

5. Social Media Advertising: Leverage paid advertising options on social media platforms to extend your reach, target specific audience segments, and drive conversions. Craft compelling ad creatives and messaging that resonate with your target audience, and optimize your campaigns based on performance data.

6. Influencer Marketing: Collaborate with influencers and brand ambassadors who align with your brand values and have a strong connection with your target audience. Influencer partnerships can help boost your brand's credibility, reach, and engagement.

7. Analytics and Performance Measurement: Regularly monitor your social media performance using platform-specific analytics tools, such as Facebook Insights or Instagram Insights. Track key performance indicators (KPIs) like engagement, reach, and conversions, and use these insights to inform data-driven optimizations and improvements.

To effectively execute social media marketing and advertising, consider the following best practices:

- Set SMART Goals: Establish specific, measurable, achievable, relevant, and time-bound (SMART) goals for your social media efforts, and align your strategies and tactics with these objectives.
- Allocate Resources Wisely: Determine the necessary resources, such as time, budget, and personnel, to effectively manage and execute your social media strategy. Prioritize platforms and initiatives that align with your goals and provide the highest return on investment (ROI).
- Test and Iterate: Conduct A/B testing and experiment with different content types, posting times, and advertising tactics to determine what works best for your brand. Continuously refine

your strategies based on data-driven insights.

- Stay Current on Trends and Platform Updates: Keep up with the latest social media trends, platform features, and algorithm updates to ensure your strategies remain effective and relevant.

In conclusion, mastering social media marketing and advertising is essential for any brand looking to excel in the digital landscape. By selecting the right platforms, developing a strategic content plan, fostering engagement, and leveraging paid advertising and influencer partnerships, you can maximize your brand's social media presence and drive tangible results.

Part 3: Content Marketing and Inbound Strategies

Content marketing and inbound strategies are powerful tools for attracting, engaging, and converting potential customers. By creating and sharing valuable content that addresses your target audience's needs and interests, you can establish your brand as a trusted expert in your industry and generate leads organically. In this part, we will explore the key elements of successful content marketing and inbound strategies, along with actionable tips for executing them effectively.

1. Content Creation: Develop high-quality, engaging, and informative content that resonates with your target audience. Experiment with various formats, such as blog posts, articles, videos, podcasts, webinars, and infographics, to cater to different user preferences and consumption habits.

2. Content Planning: Plan your content in advance using a content calendar to ensure consistency and strategic alignment with your marketing goals. Regularly brainstorm content ideas, and prioritize topics based on relevance, search volume, and audience interest.

3. SEO Integration: Incorporate SEO best practices into your content creation process, such as conducting keyword research, optimizing titles and meta descriptions, and ensuring a mobile-friendly website. This will help your content rank higher in search engine results, driving more organic traffic to your website.

4. Lead Generation and Nurturing: Use content to generate and nurture leads by offering valuable resources, such as ebooks, whitepapers, or case studies, in exchange for contact information. Implement marketing automation and email marketing to engage and nurture leads through targeted, personalized content and offers.

5. Promotion and Distribution: Amplify your content's reach and visibility by promoting it across various channels, such as social media, email marketing, and paid advertising. Leverage partnerships, influencer collaborations, and guest posting opportunities to expand your audience and boost credibility.

6. Analytics and Performance Measurement: Regularly monitor your content marketing performance using analytics tools like Google Analytics, social media insights, and email marketing metrics. Track key performance indicators (KPIs), such as traffic, engagement, and conversions, and use these insights to inform data-driven optimizations and improvements.

To effectively execute content marketing and inbound strategies, consider the following best practices:

- Set SMART Goals: Establish specific, measurable, achievable, relevant, and time-bound (SMART) goals for your content marketing efforts, and align your strategies and tactics with these objectives.

- Develop a Clear Brand Voice: Maintain a consistent brand voice and messaging across all content to reinforce your brand identity and create a cohesive experience for your audience.

- Focus on Value and Relevance: Prioritize content that provides genuine value and relevance to your target audience, addressing their pain points, interests, and needs.

- Encourage Engagement and Sharing: Create content that encourages interaction, conversation, and sharing, helping to amplify your message and foster a sense of community around your brand.

- Continuously Improve and Optimize: Regularly assess your content marketing performance, identifying areas for improvement and refining your strategies based on data-driven insights.

In conclusion, mastering content marketing and inbound strategies is essential for any brand looking to excel in the digital landscape. By creating valuable, engaging, and targeted content, promoting it effectively, and continuously monitoring and optimizing your efforts, you can attract, engage, and convert potential customers, driving growth and success for your brand.

Part 4: Email Marketing and Marketing Automation

Email marketing and marketing automation are essential components of a successful digital marketing strategy, allowing brands to maintain personalized communication with their audience and nurture leads through the sales funnel. In this part, we will discuss the key elements of effective email marketing and marketing automation strategies, along with actionable tips for executing them successfully.

1. Email List Building: Grow your email list through ethical means, such as opt-in forms on your website, content downloads, and event registrations. Ensure that your subscribers provide explicit consent to receive communications from your brand.

2. Segmentation and Personalization: Segment your email list based on factors like demographics, interests, and engagement to deliver targeted, personalized content that resonates with each subscriber. Use dynamic content and merge tags to customize email elements, such as subject lines, greetings, and offers, based on subscriber data.

3. Email Design and Content: Design visually appealing, mobile-responsive email templates that align with your brand identity. Craft compelling subject lines, concise copy, and clear calls-to-action (CTAs) to encourage engagement and conversions.

4. Email Deliverability and Compliance: Optimize your email deliverability by maintaining a clean email list, authenticating your sender domain, and following best practices for email design and content. Comply with email marketing regulations, such as the CAN-SPAM Act, GDPR, and CASL, to protect your brand's reputation and avoid penalties.

5. Marketing Automation: Implement marketing automation tools and processes to streamline and optimize your email marketing efforts. Set up automated workflows, such as welcome sequences, lead nurturing campaigns, and cart abandonment reminders, to engage subscribers with timely, relevant content based on their behaviors and actions.

6. Testing and Optimization: Regularly test and optimize your email campaigns through A/B testing, experimenting with variables like subject lines, send times, and content. Monitor key performance indicators (KPIs), such as open rates, click-through rates (CTRs), and conversions, and use these insights to inform data-driven improvements.

To effectively execute email marketing and marketing automation strategies, consider the following best practices:

- Set SMART Goals: Establish specific, measurable, achievable, relevant, and time-bound (SMART) goals for your email marketing efforts, and align your strategies and tactics with these objectives.

- Prioritize Quality Over Quantity: Focus on sending high-quality, valuable content to your subscribers, rather than overwhelming them with excessive emails. Aim to maintain a healthy balance between promotional and educational content.

- Encourage Engagement and Interaction: Design your emails to encourage engagement and interaction, such as posing questions, soliciting feedback, or using interactive elements like polls and quizzes.

- Monitor and Adapt: Continuously monitor your email marketing performance and adapt your strategies based on subscriber feedback and data-driven insights. Stay current on industry trends and best practices to ensure your efforts remain effective and relevant.

In conclusion, mastering email marketing and marketing automation is crucial for any brand looking to excel in the digital landscape. By building a strong email list, delivering personalized, engaging content, and leveraging automation tools and processes, you can nurture leads, drive conversions, and foster long-term customer relationships.

Chapter 6: Data-Driven Marketing Decisions

Part 1: Collecting and Analyzing Marketing Data

In today's competitive business environment, making data-driven marketing decisions is crucial for success. Collecting, analyzing, and interpreting marketing data allows brands to optimize their strategies, allocate resources effectively, and drive better results. In this part, we will discuss the key aspects of collecting and analyzing marketing data, along with actionable tips for leveraging data to make informed marketing decisions.

1. Data Collection Methods: Utilize various data collection methods to gather marketing data, such as web analytics, social media insights, email marketing metrics, and customer surveys. Ensure that the data collected is accurate, relevant, and timely to support your decision-making process.

2. Data Integration: Consolidate data from multiple sources into a single, unified platform or dashboard for easier analysis and interpretation. This can help you gain a holistic view of your marketing performance and identify trends, patterns, and opportunities.

3. Data Quality and Consistency: Maintain data quality and consistency by standardizing data collection and processing procedures, implementing data validation checks, and regularly cleaning and updating your data sets. This will ensure that your marketing decisions are based on reliable, accurate information.

4. Descriptive Analysis: Conduct descriptive analysis to summarize and visualize your marketing data, providing an overview of your performance across various channels and campaigns. Use tools like charts, tables, and graphs to present

your data in an easily digestible format.

5. Diagnostic Analysis: Perform diagnostic analysis to identify the root causes of your marketing performance, such as correlating specific tactics or strategies with changes in key performance indicators (KPIs). This can help you pinpoint areas for improvement and optimize your marketing efforts.

6. Predictive Analysis: Leverage predictive analysis techniques, such as regression modeling and machine learning algorithms, to forecast future marketing outcomes based on historical data. This can help you make proactive, data-driven decisions and allocate resources more effectively.

To effectively collect and analyze marketing data, consider the following best practices:

- Set SMART Goals: Establish specific, measurable, achievable, relevant, and time-bound (SMART) goals for your marketing efforts, and use data to track your progress and inform your decision-making process.

- Prioritize Relevant Data: Focus on collecting and analyzing data that is relevant to your marketing objectives and key performance indicators (KPIs). Avoid getting overwhelmed by excessive data and information that may not directly impact your decision-making process.

- Develop a Data-Driven Culture: Encourage a data-driven culture within your organization by promoting data literacy, training team members on data analysis techniques, and fostering a collaborative environment for data-driven decision-making.

- Continuously Learn and Adapt: Regularly review and update your data collection and analysis processes, incorporating new tools, techniques, and data sources as needed. Continuously learn from your data and adapt your marketing strategies based on data-driven insights.

In conclusion, collecting and analyzing marketing data is essential for making informed, data-driven marketing decisions. By prioritizing relevant data, maintaining data quality and consistency, and leveraging various data analysis techniques, you can optimize your marketing strategies, allocate resources effectively, and drive better results for your brand.

Part 2: Leveraging Analytics for Customer Insights

Gaining customer insights through analytics is crucial for creating effective marketing strategies that resonate with your target audience. By analyzing customer data, you can uncover patterns, preferences, and behaviors that inform your marketing decisions and help you better serve your customers. In this part, we will explore how to leverage analytics to gain valuable customer insights, along with actionable tips for applying these insights to your marketing efforts.

1. Customer Segmentation: Use analytics to segment your customer base based on factors like demographics, psychographics, behavioral patterns, and purchase history. By understanding the distinct characteristics of each segment, you can tailor your marketing messages and offers to better appeal to each group.

2. Customer Journey Mapping: Analyze customer data to map out the various touchpoints and stages in the customer journey, from awareness to consideration, purchase, and post-purchase. Identifying areas where customers may encounter friction or drop off can help you optimize the customer experience and improve conversion rates.

3. Sentiment Analysis: Leverage sentiment analysis tools and techniques to gauge customer emotions and opinions toward your brand, products, or services. By understanding how customers perceive your brand, you can address concerns, capitalize on positive sentiment, and improve overall brand reputation.

4. Churn Analysis: Analyze customer data to identify patterns and factors that contribute to customer churn, such as product dissatisfaction or poor customer service. By addressing

these issues and implementing strategies to improve customer retention, you can increase customer lifetime value and drive long-term growth.

5. Customer Lifetime Value (CLV) Analysis: Calculate customer lifetime value by analyzing historical transaction data and estimating the net profit attributed to a customer over their entire relationship with your brand. Understanding CLV can help you allocate marketing resources more effectively and prioritize customer segments with higher potential value.

To effectively leverage analytics for customer insights, consider the following best practices:

- Invest in Analytics Tools: Utilize robust analytics tools and platforms that enable you to collect, analyze, and visualize customer data, making it easier to derive actionable insights and make data-driven decisions.

- Encourage Cross-Functional Collaboration: Foster collaboration between marketing, sales, customer service, and other departments to share customer data and insights, enabling a more holistic understanding of customer needs and preferences.

- Test and Optimize: Continuously test and optimize your marketing strategies based on customer insights, using A/B testing, customer feedback, and performance data to refine your tactics and improve results.

- Prioritize Data Privacy: Ensure that your customer data collection and analysis practices comply with relevant data privacy regulations, such as GDPR and CCPA, to protect customer information and maintain trust in your brand.

In conclusion, leveraging analytics for customer insights is essential for creating effective marketing strategies that resonate with your target audience. By analyzing customer data, segmenting your audience, mapping customer journeys, and conducting various types of analysis, you can gain valuable insights that inform your marketing decisions and help you better serve your customers.

Part 3: A/B Testing and Optimization

A/B testing and optimization are critical components of data-driven marketing, enabling marketers to make informed decisions based on real-world performance data. By testing different variations of marketing elements and measuring their impact on key performance indicators (KPIs), you can refine your strategies and tactics to maximize results. In this part, we will discuss the importance of A/B testing and optimization, along with actionable tips for implementing these practices effectively.

1. Understanding A/B Testing: A/B testing, also known as split testing, involves comparing two or more variations of a marketing element, such as a webpage, email, or advertisement, to determine which version performs better. By measuring the performance of each variation in relation to a specific KPI, such as click-through rate or conversion rate, you can identify the most effective option and make data-driven improvements.

2. Choosing Variables to Test: Identify variables within your marketing campaigns that can be tested, such as headlines, calls-to-action (CTAs), images, or layout. Focus on testing elements that have the potential to significantly impact your KPIs and prioritize high-impact tests.

3. Designing and Implementing A/B Tests: Create multiple variations of the marketing element you want to test, ensuring that only one variable is changed at a time to isolate its impact. Use a dedicated A/B testing tool or platform to randomly assign each variation to a portion of your audience and collect performance data.

4. Analyzing Test Results: Analyze the performance data collected during your A/B test to determine which variation performed better based on your chosen KPI. Use statistical analysis, such as

calculating the confidence level and p-value, to ensure that your results are statistically significant and not due to chance.

5. Applying Test Insights: Based on your test results, implement the winning variation in your marketing campaign and continue monitoring performance to ensure that the improvements are sustained. Use the insights gained from your A/B tests to inform future marketing decisions and optimize your strategies.

To effectively leverage A/B testing and optimization, consider the following best practices:

- Establish a Testing Culture: Foster a culture of testing and optimization within your organization, encouraging team members to continuously seek opportunities for improvement and embrace data-driven decision-making.
- Plan and Prioritize Tests: Develop a strategic testing plan that outlines your testing objectives, prioritizes high-impact tests, and allocates resources effectively.
- Test Regularly and Iteratively: Conduct regular A/B tests and use the insights gained to inform ongoing optimization efforts. Approach testing as an iterative process, continuously refining your marketing strategies and tactics based on data-driven insights.
- Be Patient and Persistent: Recognize that not all A/B tests will yield immediate, dramatic results. Be patient and persistent in your testing efforts, learning from both successful and unsuccessful tests to inform future optimization strategies.

In conclusion, A/B testing and optimization are essential for data-driven marketing success, enabling you to refine your strategies and tactics based on real-world performance data. By choosing variables to test, designing and implementing tests, analyzing results, and applying insights, you can continuously improve your marketing efforts and drive better results for your brand.

Part 4: Turning Data into Actionable Insights

Collecting and analyzing data is just the beginning of the data-driven marketing process; the ultimate goal is to turn that data into actionable insights that inform your marketing strategies and drive results. In this part, we will discuss how to transform your marketing data into valuable insights and apply these insights to optimize your marketing efforts effectively.

1. Data Synthesis: Combine and synthesize data from multiple sources, such as web analytics, social media insights, and customer surveys, to gain a comprehensive understanding of your marketing performance. This holistic view can help you identify trends, patterns, and areas of opportunity.

2. Identifying Key Insights: Review your marketing data and identify key insights that can inform your marketing decisions. Look for patterns and correlations that reveal customer preferences, behaviors, and pain points, as well as areas where your marketing strategies are underperforming or excelling.

3. Prioritizing Insights: Not all insights will have the same impact on your marketing efforts. Prioritize the most important insights based on their potential to drive results and align with your marketing objectives.

4. Developing Action Plans: Translate your insights into actionable steps that can be implemented to optimize your marketing strategies. Create detailed action plans outlining the specific tactics, resources, and timelines required to address the insights identified.

5. Implementing and Monitoring: Execute your action plans and closely monitor the impact of your changes on your marketing

performance. Use data to assess whether your optimizations are driving the desired results and continue refining your strategies based on ongoing insights.

To effectively turn data into actionable insights, consider the following best practices:

- Foster a Data-Driven Culture: Encourage a data-driven mindset within your organization, promoting data literacy, training team members on data analysis techniques, and fostering a collaborative environment for data-driven decision-making.

- Utilize Advanced Analytics Tools: Leverage advanced analytics tools and platforms that enable you to collect, analyze, and visualize data, making it easier to derive actionable insights and make data-driven decisions.

- Continuously Learn and Adapt: Regularly review and update your data collection and analysis processes, incorporating new tools, techniques, and data sources as needed. Continuously learn from your data and adapt your marketing strategies based on data-driven insights.

- Maintain Data Quality and Integrity: Ensure that your data collection and analysis practices maintain data quality and integrity by standardizing processes, implementing data validation checks, and regularly cleaning and updating your data sets.

In conclusion, turning data into actionable insights is essential for optimizing your marketing efforts and driving better results. By synthesizing data, identifying key insights, prioritizing their importance, developing action plans, and implementing changes, you can transform your marketing data into valuable insights that inform your marketing decisions and help you achieve your objectives.

Chapter 7: Creative Marketing Campaigns

Part 1: Elements of a Successful Marketing Campaign

A successful marketing campaign captures the attention of your target audience, communicates your brand message effectively, and drives measurable results. In this part, we will discuss the essential elements of a successful marketing campaign, providing a foundation for creating creative and impactful campaigns that resonate with your audience.

1. Clear Objectives: Establish well-defined objectives for your marketing campaign, ensuring that they align with your overall marketing and business goals. Clear objectives provide a framework for evaluating campaign performance and measuring success.

2. Target Audience: Identify and understand your target audience, including their demographics, psychographics, preferences, and pain points. A deep understanding of your audience enables you to create personalized and relevant marketing messages that resonate with them.

3. Unique Selling Proposition (USP): Clearly communicate your brand's unique selling proposition, highlighting the distinct benefits and value that your product or service offers to your target audience. Your USP should differentiate your brand from competitors and provide a compelling reason for customers to choose you.

4. Compelling Creative Concepts: Develop creative concepts that capture the attention of your audience and evoke an emotional response. Strive to create memorable and impactful marketing materials that communicate your brand message effectively and

leave a lasting impression.

5. Integrated Marketing Communications: Ensure that your marketing campaign utilizes a mix of marketing channels and tactics, such as social media, email, content marketing, and public relations, to deliver a consistent and cohesive brand message across all touchpoints.

6. Testing and Optimization: Continuously test and optimize your marketing campaign, using data-driven insights to refine your messaging, creative elements, and marketing tactics. A/B testing and ongoing analysis can help you identify areas of improvement and maximize campaign results.

7. Measurement and Analysis: Establish key performance indicators (KPIs) that align with your campaign objectives, and regularly measure and analyze campaign performance to gauge success. Use data-driven insights to make informed decisions about future marketing efforts and allocate resources effectively.

To create a successful marketing campaign, consider the following best practices:

- Collaborate and Brainstorm: Foster a collaborative environment within your marketing team, encouraging open communication and idea-sharing during the creative process. Brainstorming sessions can help you generate fresh, innovative concepts for your marketing campaign.
- Be Consistent with Your Brand: Ensure that your marketing campaign aligns with your overall brand identity, maintaining a consistent look, feel, and tone across all marketing materials and channels.
- Embrace Storytelling: Leverage the power of storytelling to create emotional connections with your audience and

communicate your brand message effectively. A compelling narrative can make your marketing campaign more memorable and impactful.

- Monitor Trends and Competitors: Stay up-to-date with industry trends and competitor campaigns, using this knowledge to inform your marketing strategy and ensure that your campaign remains fresh and relevant.

In conclusion, a successful marketing campaign incorporates clear objectives, a well-defined target audience, a unique selling proposition, compelling creative concepts, integrated marketing communications, testing and optimization, and measurement and analysis. By focusing on these essential elements, you can create creative and impactful marketing campaigns that resonate with your audience and drive results for your brand.

Part 2: Developing a Campaign Concept

Developing a compelling campaign concept is crucial for capturing your audience's attention and effectively communicating your brand message. A strong concept sets the foundation for a successful marketing campaign. In this part, we will discuss the process of developing a campaign concept, providing actionable tips and guidelines to help you create an impactful marketing campaign.

1. Research and Insights: Begin by conducting thorough research to gain a deeper understanding of your target audience, industry trends, and competitor activities. Analyze your marketing data to identify key insights that can inform your campaign concept and ensure that your message resonates with your audience.

2. Define Campaign Objectives: Establish clear objectives for your marketing campaign, ensuring that they align with your overall marketing and business goals. These objectives will guide your campaign development process and help you evaluate the success of your campaign.

3. Brainstorm Ideas: Gather your marketing team and engage in brainstorming sessions to generate a wide range of ideas for your campaign concept. Encourage open communication, creative thinking, and collaboration to foster an environment where innovative ideas can flourish.

4. Evaluate and Refine Ideas: Review the ideas generated during the brainstorming sessions and evaluate them based on their potential to meet your campaign objectives, resonate with your target audience, and differentiate your brand from competitors. Refine and iterate the most promising ideas, combining and building upon them to create a unique and compelling campaign concept.

5. Create a Campaign Narrative: Develop a narrative that ties your campaign concept together, incorporating storytelling elements to evoke an emotional response and create a memorable experience for your audience. Your narrative should clearly communicate your brand message and unique selling proposition.

6. Design Campaign Assets: Create visually appealing and impactful campaign assets, such as images, videos, and graphics, that bring your campaign concept to life. Ensure that these assets are consistent with your overall brand identity and effectively communicate your campaign narrative.

7. Develop a Multichannel Marketing Plan: Develop a marketing plan that incorporates a mix of marketing channels and tactics, such as social media, email, content marketing, and public relations, to deliver a consistent and cohesive brand message across all touchpoints. This integrated approach helps you reach your audience through various channels and maximizes the impact of your campaign.

8. Test and Optimize: Continuously test and optimize your campaign assets and marketing tactics, using data-driven insights to refine your messaging and creative elements. A/B testing and ongoing analysis can help you identify areas of improvement and maximize campaign results.

In conclusion, developing a campaign concept involves conducting research, defining objectives, brainstorming ideas, evaluating and refining ideas, creating a narrative, designing campaign assets, developing a multichannel marketing plan, and testing and optimizing your campaign. By following these steps, you can create a compelling campaign concept that effectively captures your audience's attention, communicates your brand message, and drives measurable results.

Part 3: Executing and Managing Campaigns

Once you've developed a compelling campaign concept, the next step is to execute and manage the campaign effectively. Proper execution and management are crucial for maximizing the impact of your marketing efforts and achieving your campaign objectives. In this part, we will discuss best practices for executing and managing marketing campaigns, ensuring that your campaign runs smoothly and delivers the desired results.

1. Develop a Detailed Campaign Plan: Create a comprehensive campaign plan that outlines the specific marketing tactics, channels, timelines, and resources required for each stage of the campaign. This plan will serve as a roadmap for your team, ensuring that everyone is aligned on objectives, responsibilities, and expectations.

2. Assign Roles and Responsibilities: Clearly define the roles and responsibilities of each team member involved in the campaign, ensuring that everyone understands their tasks and deadlines. This clarity helps to prevent misunderstandings and ensures that each aspect of the campaign is executed efficiently.

3. Set Up Tracking and Measurement: Establish key performance indicators (KPIs) that align with your campaign objectives, and set up tracking systems to measure your campaign's performance. This data-driven approach enables you to evaluate the success of your campaign, identify areas for improvement, and make informed decisions about future marketing efforts.

4. Execute the Campaign: With your plan in place, execute each aspect of your campaign according to the timeline and resources outlined in your campaign plan. Ensure that your team members are aware of their deadlines and responsibilities, and monitor their progress to ensure that tasks are completed on time and

within budget.

5. Monitor and Adjust: Regularly monitor the performance of your campaign, using data-driven insights to identify areas where adjustments may be necessary. Be prepared to make real-time adjustments to your marketing tactics, creative assets, and messaging as needed, based on your ongoing analysis of campaign performance.

6. Communicate and Collaborate: Foster open communication and collaboration among your team members, encouraging them to share their insights, challenges, and successes throughout the campaign. This collaborative approach helps to identify potential issues early on and enables your team to work together to address them effectively.

7. Review and Evaluate: Once your campaign has concluded, conduct a thorough evaluation of its performance, using your KPIs and data-driven insights to assess its success. Identify areas where your campaign excelled and areas where improvements could be made, using these learnings to inform future marketing efforts.

8. Share Results and Lessons Learned: Share the results of your campaign evaluation with your team and other stakeholders, highlighting successes, challenges, and key learnings. This transparency helps to foster a culture of continuous improvement and ensures that your team is well-prepared for future marketing campaigns.

In conclusion, executing and managing marketing campaigns effectively involves developing a detailed campaign plan, assigning roles and responsibilities, setting up tracking and measurement, executing the campaign, monitoring and adjusting, communicating and collaborating, reviewing and evaluating, and sharing results and lessons learned. By following these best practices, you can ensure that your marketing campaign runs smoothly and delivers the desired results for your brand.

Part 4: Measuring Campaign Effectiveness and ROI

Measuring the effectiveness and return on investment (ROI) of your marketing campaign is crucial for evaluating its success and informing future marketing decisions. A data-driven approach helps you understand which aspects of your campaign performed well and which areas could be improved. In this part, we will discuss best practices for measuring campaign effectiveness and ROI, ensuring that you have the necessary insights to optimize your marketing efforts.

1. Define Key Performance Indicators (KPIs): Establish KPIs that align with your campaign objectives and are relevant to your marketing tactics and channels. These KPIs will provide a framework for measuring campaign performance and evaluating success.

2. Set Up Tracking and Analytics: Implement tracking and analytics tools to capture data related to your KPIs. Ensure that these tools are set up correctly to provide accurate insights into your campaign performance.

3. Monitor Performance in Real-Time: Regularly review your campaign data and monitor performance in real-time. This ongoing analysis enables you to identify trends, spot potential issues, and make data-driven decisions to optimize your campaign.

4. Calculate ROI: Calculate the return on investment for your marketing campaign by comparing the cost of your marketing efforts to the revenue generated as a result. This calculation helps you understand the financial impact of your campaign and informs decisions about future marketing investments.

5. Conduct A/B Testing: Use A/B testing to compare the performance of different creative assets, messaging, and marketing tactics. This data-driven approach helps you identify the most effective elements of your campaign and optimize your marketing efforts accordingly.

6. Analyze Performance by Channel and Tactic: Break down your campaign performance by marketing channel and tactic to understand which aspects of your campaign were most effective. This granular analysis can help you allocate resources more effectively in future campaigns and improve overall marketing performance.

7. Evaluate Qualitative Metrics: In addition to quantitative KPIs, consider qualitative metrics such as brand awareness, customer sentiment, and overall customer experience. These metrics can provide valuable insights into the impact of your campaign on your target audience and help you refine your marketing approach.

8. Review and Learn: Conduct a comprehensive review of your campaign performance, evaluating both quantitative and qualitative metrics. Identify areas where your campaign excelled and areas where improvements could be made, using these learnings to inform future marketing efforts.

9. Share Results and Insights: Communicate the results of your campaign evaluation with your team and other stakeholders, highlighting successes, challenges, and key learnings. This transparency helps to foster a culture of continuous improvement and ensures that your team is well-prepared for future marketing campaigns.

In conclusion, measuring campaign effectiveness and ROI

involves defining KPIs, setting up tracking and analytics, monitoring performance in real-time, calculating ROI, conducting A/B testing, analyzing performance by channel and tactic, evaluating qualitative metrics, reviewing and learning, and sharing results and insights. By following these best practices, you can gain valuable insights into your marketing campaign's performance, optimize your marketing efforts, and maximize the impact of your marketing investments.

Chapter 8: Building Long-Term Customer Relationships

Part 1: The Importance of Customer Retention

Building long-term customer relationships is essential for the sustainable growth and success of any business. Customer retention is a vital aspect of these relationships, as retaining existing customers is often more cost-effective and profitable than acquiring new ones. In this part, we will discuss the importance of customer retention and its impact on your business's growth and bottom line.

1. Cost-Effectiveness: Acquiring new customers can be expensive, as it often involves significant marketing and advertising efforts. Retaining existing customers is generally more cost-effective, as it requires less investment in marketing and can be achieved through excellent customer service and consistent value delivery.

2. Increased Customer Lifetime Value: When you retain customers, their lifetime value (CLV) increases, as they continue to make purchases and engage with your brand over time. This increased value translates to higher revenue and profitability for your business.

3. Higher Profitability: Studies have shown that a small increase in customer retention rates can lead to a significant increase in profit. Loyal customers often make larger and more frequent purchases, leading to higher overall revenue.

4. Customer Advocacy: Satisfied and loyal customers are more likely to recommend your brand to their friends and family, acting as brand advocates. This word-of-mouth marketing can help drive new customer acquisition and enhance your brand's reputation.

5. Reduced Churn Rate: By focusing on customer retention, you can reduce the rate at which customers discontinue their relationship with your brand, or "churn." A lower churn rate is essential for maintaining a stable customer base and ensuring sustainable growth.

6. Valuable Feedback: Loyal customers are more likely to provide feedback on your products and services, helping you identify areas for improvement and opportunities for innovation. This feedback can be invaluable for refining your product offerings and customer experience.

7. Competitive Advantage: A strong focus on customer retention can help differentiate your brand from competitors, as customers are more likely to remain loyal to a brand that consistently meets or exceeds their expectations.

8. Stronger Brand Community: Building long-term relationships with your customers can foster a sense of community around your brand, leading to increased customer engagement and loyalty.

In conclusion, customer retention is crucial for the sustainable growth and success of any business. It offers numerous benefits, including cost-effectiveness, increased customer lifetime value, higher profitability, customer advocacy, reduced churn rate, valuable feedback, competitive advantage, and a stronger brand community. By focusing on retaining existing customers, you can maximize the value of your customer relationships and drive long-term success for your business.

Part 2: Customer Relationship Management (CRM) Strategies

Customer Relationship Management (CRM) is a strategic approach to managing and improving interactions with customers throughout their lifecycle. CRM strategies help businesses build long-term relationships with customers by understanding their needs, preferences, and behaviors, enabling more personalized and relevant experiences. In this part, we will discuss various CRM strategies that can help you strengthen your customer relationships and boost customer retention.

1. Implement CRM Software: CRM software can help you centralize and manage customer data, enabling you to better understand your customers' preferences, habits, and interactions with your brand. This data-driven approach allows you to make more informed decisions about your marketing, sales, and customer service efforts.

2. Personalize Customer Experiences: Use the data gathered through your CRM software to create personalized experiences for your customers, whether through targeted marketing campaigns, tailored product recommendations, or customized communications. Personalization can help improve customer satisfaction and encourage loyalty.

3. Segment Your Customer Base: Divide your customers into distinct groups based on their characteristics, behaviors, or preferences. This segmentation enables you to develop targeted marketing strategies and deliver more relevant content to each customer segment.

4. Engage Customers Across Channels: Interact with your customers across multiple channels, including email, social media, phone, and in-person. This omnichannel approach ensures that customers have a consistent experience with your brand,

regardless of the channel they use to engage with you.

5. Offer Exceptional Customer Service: Provide outstanding customer service to address customer concerns, answer questions, and resolve issues promptly. An excellent customer service experience can significantly impact customer satisfaction and loyalty.

6. Develop a Loyalty Program: Implement a loyalty program that rewards customers for their continued patronage, encouraging repeat purchases and long-term engagement. Offer exclusive discounts, perks, or rewards for loyal customers to show your appreciation for their business.

7. Solicit Customer Feedback: Regularly ask your customers for feedback on your products, services, and overall customer experience. Use this feedback to identify areas for improvement and implement changes that enhance customer satisfaction.

8. Monitor and Analyze Customer Data: Continuously analyze your CRM data to identify trends, patterns, and opportunities for improvement. Use these insights to refine your marketing, sales, and customer service strategies, ensuring that you are continually meeting or exceeding customer expectations.

9. Nurture Long-Term Relationships: Focus on building long-term relationships with your customers by consistently providing value, excellent service, and relevant experiences. This long-term approach can help you maintain a stable customer base and drive sustainable growth.

In conclusion, effective CRM strategies involve implementing CRM software, personalizing customer experiences, segmenting your customer base, engaging customers across channels, offering exceptional customer service, developing a loyalty program, soliciting customer feedback, monitoring and analyzing customer data, and nurturing long-term relationships. By incorporating these strategies into your business, you can strengthen your customer relationships, boost customer retention, and drive long-term success.

Part 3: Personalization and Customization in Marketing

Personalization and customization play an increasingly important role in modern marketing strategies, as they enable businesses to deliver more relevant and engaging experiences to their customers. By tailoring content, offers, and interactions to individual customer preferences and behaviors, businesses can create more meaningful connections and foster long-term loyalty. In this part, we will discuss the importance of personalization and customization in marketing and how to implement these strategies effectively.

1. Understand Your Customers: To personalize and customize your marketing efforts, you must first understand your customers' needs, preferences, and behaviors. Collect and analyze data from various sources, including CRM systems, social media, web analytics, and customer surveys, to gain insights into your customers.

2. Segment Your Audience: Divide your customer base into segments based on their characteristics, preferences, and behaviors. This segmentation allows you to tailor your marketing efforts to better resonate with each group.

3. Create Personalized Content: Develop content that speaks to the unique needs and interests of each customer segment. Personalized content can include targeted blog posts, videos, social media posts, or email campaigns that cater to specific customer preferences or address particular pain points.

4. Implement Customized Product Recommendations: Use customer data and insights to offer tailored product or service recommendations to individual customers. These recommendations can be based on factors such as browsing history, past purchases, or preferences indicated through surveys

or feedback.

5. Leverage Marketing Automation: Marketing automation tools can help you deliver personalized content and offers to customers based on their interactions with your brand. Utilize these tools to automate processes such as email campaigns, social media posting, and ad targeting, ensuring that your customers receive timely and relevant content.

6. Utilize Dynamic Content: Incorporate dynamic content into your marketing materials, which automatically adapts based on the viewer's characteristics or behavior. This can include elements such as personalized email greetings, dynamic website content, or personalized ad creative.

7. Offer Customized Services: Provide tailored services to your customers, such as personalized consultations, customized product bundles, or individualized support, to address their unique needs and create a more memorable customer experience.

8. Measure and Optimize: Continuously monitor the performance of your personalization and customization efforts, using metrics such as engagement, conversion, and customer satisfaction. Use these insights to optimize your strategies, ensuring that you are consistently delivering relevant and engaging experiences to your customers.

9. Balance Personalization with Privacy: While personalization can improve customer experiences, it's essential to balance this with respecting customer privacy. Be transparent about your data collection practices, allow customers to control their data preferences, and ensure that you are complying with relevant data privacy regulations.

In conclusion, personalization and customization in marketing involve understanding your customers, segmenting your audience, creating personalized content, implementing customized product recommendations, leveraging marketing automation, utilizing dynamic content, offering customized services, measuring and optimizing, and balancing personalization with privacy. By incorporating these strategies into your marketing efforts, you can create more meaningful connections with your customers, foster long-term loyalty, and drive growth for your business.

Part 4: Loyalty Programs and Rewards

Loyalty programs and rewards are powerful tools for building long-term customer relationships and encouraging repeat business. These programs offer incentives to customers for their continued patronage, fostering a sense of loyalty and connection to your brand. In this part, we will discuss the benefits of loyalty programs and rewards and explore strategies for designing and implementing effective programs.

1. Benefits of Loyalty Programs and Rewards:
   - Increase customer retention rates
   - Boost customer lifetime value (CLV)
   - Encourage repeat purchases
   - Strengthen brand loyalty
   - Attract new customers through referrals
   - Enhance customer engagement
   - Differentiate your brand from competitors
   - Collect valuable customer data and insights

2. Types of Loyalty Programs:
   - Points-based programs: Customers earn points for purchases or other actions, which can be redeemed for rewards or discounts.
   - Tiered programs: Customers receive increasing benefits as they reach higher tiers based on their spending or engagement levels.
   - Cashback programs: Customers receive a percentage of their spending back in the form of cash or store credit.
   - Membership programs: Customers pay a fee to access exclusive benefits and perks.

3. Designing an Effective Loyalty Program:

- Align with your brand values: Ensure your program reflects your brand's unique identity and values.

- Keep it simple: Design a program that is easy for customers to understand and participate in.

- Offer meaningful rewards: Provide rewards that are valuable and relevant to your customers, such as discounts, exclusive products, or special experiences.

- Encourage engagement: Incentivize actions beyond purchases, such as social media sharing, referrals, or product reviews, to foster deeper customer connections.

- Communicate regularly: Keep customers informed about their rewards status, program updates, and special offers through targeted communications.

4. Implementing and Managing Your Loyalty Program:

- Choose the right technology: Select a loyalty program platform or software that supports your program's structure, integrates with your existing systems, and provides analytics and reporting features.

- Train your staff: Ensure that employees understand the program, its benefits, and how to communicate its value to customers effectively.

- Promote your program: Market your loyalty program through various channels, such as in-store signage, email, social media, and your website, to attract new members and remind existing members of its benefits.

- Analyze and optimize: Continuously monitor your program's performance using key metrics, such as retention rate, average transaction value, and program participation. Use these insights to optimize your program and maximize its impact on customer loyalty and satisfaction.

In conclusion, loyalty programs and rewards can significantly enhance your ability to build long-term customer relationships and drive repeat business. By designing a program that aligns with your brand values, offers meaningful rewards, encourages engagement, and is effectively implemented and managed, you can foster a loyal customer base and drive sustainable growth for your business.

Chapter 9: Ethical Marketing Practices

Part 1: The Role of Ethics in Marketing

Ethics play a crucial role in marketing, as they guide the principles and values that shape a company's marketing practices. Ethical marketing not only benefits customers by ensuring that they are treated fairly and with respect, but it also strengthens a company's reputation and fosters trust among its target audience. In this part, we will discuss the role of ethics in marketing and the importance of adhering to ethical principles in your marketing strategies.

1. Understanding Ethical Marketing: Ethical marketing involves making marketing decisions and implementing practices that respect customers, competitors, and the broader community. It encompasses various aspects, such as truthful advertising, transparent pricing, protecting consumer privacy, and promoting socially responsible behaviors.

2. The Importance of Ethics in Marketing:

   - Build customer trust: Ethical marketing practices demonstrate to customers that your company values their well-being and is committed to acting in their best interests.

   - Enhance brand reputation: A company with a reputation for ethical marketing is more likely to attract customers who value transparency, honesty, and social responsibility.

   - Foster customer loyalty: Customers are more likely to remain loyal to companies that treat them fairly and prioritize their needs.

   - Encourage positive word-of-mouth: Ethical marketing practices can lead to positive customer experiences, which can generate referrals and recommendations.

- Comply with regulations: Adhering to ethical guidelines can help companies avoid legal issues and penalties related to false advertising, unfair pricing, or unethical practices.

3. Principles of Ethical Marketing:

- Honesty and transparency: Be truthful and accurate in your marketing messages, and avoid misleading or deceptive practices.

- Respect for privacy: Protect customer data and respect their privacy preferences, ensuring that you comply with relevant data privacy regulations.

- Fairness and equity: Treat customers fairly, regardless of their demographic characteristics or socioeconomic status, and avoid discriminatory practices.

- Social responsibility: Consider the broader social and environmental impacts of your marketing activities, and strive to promote positive change through your marketing efforts.

4. Implementing Ethical Marketing Practices:

- Develop a code of ethics: Establish a code of ethics that outlines your company's commitment to ethical marketing practices and provides guidelines for employees to follow.

- Train employees: Provide training and resources to help employees understand the importance of ethical marketing and how to apply ethical principles in their daily work.

- Encourage open communication: Create an environment in which employees feel comfortable raising ethical concerns or discussing potential ethical dilemmas.

- Monitor and enforce compliance: Regularly review your marketing practices to ensure that they adhere to your company's ethical guidelines, and address any violations promptly and effectively.

In conclusion, the role of ethics in marketing is essential for creating trust, enhancing brand reputation, fostering customer loyalty, encouraging positive word-of-mouth, and ensuring regulatory compliance. By adhering to ethical principles, such as honesty, transparency, respect for privacy, fairness, and social responsibility, and implementing ethical marketing practices, your company can build strong, long-lasting relationships with customers and drive sustainable business growth.

Part 2: Navigating Legal and Regulatory Compliance

Legal and regulatory compliance is a critical aspect of ethical marketing, as it ensures that companies adhere to the laws and regulations governing advertising, consumer protection, privacy, and other marketing-related areas. In this part, we will discuss the importance of legal and regulatory compliance in marketing and provide guidance on how to navigate these requirements effectively.

1. The Importance of Legal and Regulatory Compliance:

- Protect consumers: Compliance with marketing laws and regulations helps ensure that consumers are treated fairly and are provided with accurate information about products and services.

- Preserve your company's reputation: Adhering to legal and regulatory requirements helps maintain your company's credibility and demonstrates a commitment to ethical business practices.

- Avoid fines and penalties: Non-compliance can result in significant financial penalties, legal action, and reputational damage.

- Foster a culture of compliance: Ensuring legal and regulatory compliance in your marketing activities contributes to a company-wide culture that values ethical behavior and accountability.

2. Key Areas of Legal and Regulatory Compliance in Marketing:

- Advertising and promotions: Ensure that your advertising and promotional materials are truthful, accurate, and do not mislead or deceive consumers. Comply with specific regulations related to advertising claims, endorsements, testimonials, and special offers.

- Consumer protection: Adhere to consumer protection laws

that govern pricing, product safety, warranties, and refunds, ensuring that customers are treated fairly and their rights are respected.

- Privacy and data protection: Comply with data protection and privacy laws, such as the General Data Protection Regulation (GDPR) or the California Consumer Privacy Act (CCPA), to protect customer data and respect their privacy preferences.

- Intellectual property: Respect the intellectual property rights of others, including copyrights, trademarks, and patents, and ensure that your marketing materials do not infringe upon these rights.

3. Strategies for Navigating Legal and Regulatory Compliance:

- Develop a compliance program: Establish a comprehensive compliance program that outlines your company's commitment to adhering to legal and regulatory requirements and provides guidelines for employees to follow.

- Assign responsibility: Designate a compliance officer or team to oversee your company's marketing compliance efforts and ensure that employees understand their responsibilities in maintaining compliance.

- Train employees: Provide training and resources to help employees understand the legal and regulatory requirements relevant to their marketing roles and how to apply these requirements in their daily work.

- Conduct regular audits: Periodically review your marketing practices, materials, and data handling processes to ensure ongoing compliance with applicable laws and regulations.

- Seek expert advice: Consult with legal and regulatory experts, as needed, to help you navigate complex compliance issues and stay informed about changes in laws and regulations that may impact your marketing activities.

In conclusion, navigating legal and regulatory compliance in marketing is crucial for protecting consumers, preserving your company's reputation, avoiding fines and penalties, and fostering a culture of compliance. By focusing on key areas such as advertising and promotions, consumer protection, privacy and data protection, and intellectual property, and employing strategies such as developing a compliance program, assigning responsibility, training employees, conducting regular audits, and seeking expert advice, your company can effectively manage its compliance obligations and uphold ethical marketing practices.

Part 3: Socially Responsible Marketing

Socially responsible marketing involves considering the broader social and environmental impacts of your marketing activities and striving to promote positive change through your marketing efforts. It reflects a company's commitment to corporate social responsibility (CSR) and its desire to contribute to the well-being of its customers, the community, and the environment. In this part, we will discuss the principles of socially responsible marketing and provide guidance on how to incorporate these principles into your marketing strategies.

1. Principles of Socially Responsible Marketing:

   - Promote sustainability: Strive to reduce the environmental impact of your marketing activities and encourage sustainable consumption by promoting eco-friendly products and practices.

   - Support community well-being: Use your marketing efforts to address social issues, support local communities, and contribute to charitable causes that align with your company's values and mission.

   - Encourage ethical consumption: Promote products and services that are produced and delivered ethically, with respect for human rights, fair labor practices, and animal welfare.

   - Foster diversity and inclusion: Ensure that your marketing messages and imagery represent diverse perspectives and are inclusive of different cultural backgrounds, age groups, genders, and abilities.

2. Strategies for Implementing Socially Responsible Marketing:

   - Align with your brand values: Ensure that your socially responsible marketing initiatives reflect your company's core values and are authentic to your brand identity.

   - Engage stakeholders: Collaborate with employees, customers, suppliers, and community members to identify social and environmental issues that are relevant to your business and develop marketing initiatives that address these concerns.

- Communicate your impact: Share the stories and successes of your socially responsible marketing efforts through various marketing channels, such as your website, social media, and email campaigns, to build awareness and inspire others to take action.

- Measure and report progress: Monitor the impact of your socially responsible marketing initiatives using key performance indicators (KPIs) and share your progress with stakeholders through annual CSR reports or other communications.

3. Examples of Socially Responsible Marketing Initiatives:

- Cause-related marketing: Partner with a nonprofit organization or cause to raise awareness and funds through joint marketing campaigns, such as donating a portion of sales to the cause or sponsoring community events.

- Green marketing: Promote eco-friendly products and services, highlight your company's environmental initiatives, and encourage customers to adopt sustainable behaviors, such as recycling or conserving energy.

- Fair trade marketing: Support fair trade practices by sourcing products from suppliers that adhere to ethical labor standards and promoting these products to your customers.

- Inclusive marketing: Create marketing campaigns that celebrate diversity and inclusion, featuring individuals from various backgrounds and showcasing products or services that cater to a diverse audience.

In conclusion, socially responsible marketing plays a vital role in demonstrating your company's commitment to corporate social responsibility and contributing to the well-being of your customers, the community, and the environment. By adopting the principles of socially responsible marketing, such as promoting sustainability, supporting community well-being, encouraging ethical consumption, and fostering diversity and inclusion, and implementing strategies like aligning with your brand values, engaging stakeholders, communicating your impact, and measuring progress, your company can make a positive difference and strengthen its reputation as a responsible and ethical business.

Part 4: Building Trust through Transparency and Authenticity

Trust is the foundation of strong customer relationships and long-term marketing success. By embracing transparency and authenticity in your marketing efforts, you can establish trust with your target audience and create a loyal customer base. In this part, we will discuss the importance of transparency and authenticity in marketing and provide guidance on how to build trust with your customers through these principles.

1. The Importance of Transparency and Authenticity in Marketing:

- Enhance credibility: Being transparent and authentic in your marketing efforts demonstrates your company's commitment to honesty, integrity, and ethical business practices, which can enhance your brand's credibility.

- Foster customer loyalty: Customers are more likely to remain loyal to brands that are open, honest, and genuine in their marketing communications.

- Encourage positive word-of-mouth: Transparency and authenticity can lead to positive customer experiences, which can generate referrals and recommendations.

- Mitigate reputational risk: By being transparent and authentic, you can reduce the risk of negative publicity and reputational damage resulting from deceptive or unethical marketing practices.

2. Strategies for Building Trust through Transparency and Authenticity:

- Be honest in your marketing messages: Ensure that your marketing materials are accurate, truthful, and do not mislead or deceive customers. Avoid making exaggerated claims or promises that you cannot fulfill.

- Disclose relevant information: Provide customers with the information they need to make informed purchasing decisions, such as product specifications, pricing details, and any applicable terms and conditions.

- Be open about your business practices: Share information about your company's operations, supply chain, and ethical standards to demonstrate your commitment to responsible business practices.

- Share your company's story: Communicate your company's history, mission, and values to help customers understand the people and purpose behind your brand.

- Show vulnerability and humility: Acknowledge your company's mistakes or shortcomings and demonstrate a willingness to learn and improve.

3. Examples of Transparent and Authentic Marketing Initiatives:

- Product transparency: Clearly disclose product ingredients, materials, or sourcing information to help customers understand the environmental, social, and ethical implications of their purchases.

- Transparent pricing: Provide clear and detailed pricing information, including any fees, taxes, or shipping charges, so customers know exactly what they are paying for.

- Authentic storytelling: Use real-life stories, testimonials, and case studies to demonstrate the impact of your products or services on customers' lives, showcasing both the successes and the challenges.

- Open dialogue: Encourage open communication with your customers by responding to their questions, concerns, and feedback on social media, review platforms, and other communication channels.

In conclusion, building trust through transparency and

authenticity is essential for establishing strong customer relationships and driving long-term marketing success. By embracing strategies such as being honest in your marketing messages, disclosing relevant information, being open about your business practices, sharing your company's story, and showing vulnerability and humility, your company can foster trust, enhance credibility, encourage customer loyalty, and mitigate reputational risk.

Chapter 10: Future Trends in Marketing

Part 1: The Growing Role of Artificial Intelligence and Machine Learning

As technology continues to evolve, artificial intelligence (AI) and machine learning (ML) are playing increasingly prominent roles in marketing. These advanced technologies can help marketers optimize their efforts, gain deeper customer insights, and deliver more personalized and relevant experiences. In this part, we will discuss the growing role of AI and ML in marketing and explore some of the ways these technologies are shaping the future of the industry.

1. The Impact of AI and ML on Marketing:

- Improved data analysis: AI and ML can process and analyze vast amounts of marketing data quickly and efficiently, enabling marketers to uncover hidden patterns, trends, and insights that would be difficult to identify manually.

- Enhanced personalization: By analyzing customer behavior and preferences, AI and ML can help marketers create highly personalized marketing campaigns that resonate with individual consumers and drive engagement.

- Automation and efficiency: AI-powered tools can automate many routine marketing tasks, such as content generation, email marketing, and social media management, freeing up time for marketers to focus on more strategic initiatives.

- Predictive analytics: ML algorithms can analyze historical data to predict future customer behaviors, preferences, and trends, enabling marketers to make more informed decisions and optimize their campaigns.

2. Examples of AI and ML Applications in Marketing:

- Chatbots and virtual assistants: AI-powered chatbots and virtual assistants can provide real-time customer support, answer questions, and guide users through the purchasing process, improving the overall customer experience.

- Content generation and curation: AI-driven tools can create and curate content for marketing purposes, such as blog posts, social media updates, and even video scripts, based on specific parameters and audience preferences.

- Customer segmentation and targeting: ML algorithms can analyze customer data to identify meaningful segments and target these groups with tailored marketing messages, offers, and promotions.

- Sentiment analysis: AI can analyze social media and online reviews to gauge consumer sentiment toward a brand, product, or service, providing valuable feedback for marketers to refine their strategies.

3. Preparing for the Future of AI and ML in Marketing:

- Stay informed: Keep up with the latest developments in AI and ML technologies and their applications in marketing, ensuring that you are aware of emerging trends and best practices.

- Invest in skills development: Encourage your marketing team to develop skills in AI and ML, such as data analysis, programming, and machine learning techniques.

- Experiment with AI-powered tools: Test and evaluate different AI-driven marketing tools and platforms to determine which ones best meet your needs and can help you achieve your marketing objectives.

- Collaborate with experts: Partner with AI and ML experts or consultancies to leverage their knowledge and expertise in implementing these technologies in your marketing efforts.

In conclusion, the growing role of AI and ML in marketing

is set to transform the industry, offering new opportunities for improved data analysis, personalization, automation, and predictive analytics. By staying informed about these emerging technologies, investing in skills development, experimenting with AI-powered tools, and collaborating with experts, marketers can effectively harness the power of AI and ML to enhance their marketing strategies and drive future success.

Part 2: The Impact of Augmented and Virtual Reality

Augmented reality (AR) and virtual reality (VR) are rapidly changing the landscape of marketing, offering new and immersive ways for brands to engage with their customers. These technologies provide innovative opportunities to create interactive and experiential marketing campaigns that can captivate audiences and enhance brand experiences. In this part, we will discuss the impact of AR and VR on marketing and explore some of the ways these technologies are shaping the future of the industry.

1. The Impact of AR and VR on Marketing:

   - Enhanced customer experiences: AR and VR allow marketers to create immersive and interactive experiences that engage customers on a deeper level, fostering emotional connections with the brand.

   - Improved product visualization: These technologies enable customers to visualize products in realistic, three-dimensional environments, making it easier for them to imagine how the products will look and function in real-life settings.

   - Increased brand awareness and engagement: Innovative AR and VR marketing campaigns can generate buzz and drive social sharing, helping brands reach new audiences and increase engagement.

   - Personalized experiences: AR and VR can be tailored to individual preferences and behaviors, providing customized experiences that cater to each customer's unique needs and interests.

2. Examples of AR and VR Applications in Marketing:

   - Virtual product demonstrations: Brands can use VR to showcase their products in immersive, 3D environments, allowing customers to explore features and functionality in a virtual setting.

- Augmented retail experiences: AR can be used in retail settings to provide customers with additional product information, virtual fitting rooms, or interactive store maps.

- Immersive branded content: Brands can create engaging AR and VR content, such as games, interactive videos, or virtual tours, to promote their products and services.

- Live event experiences: AR and VR can be used to enhance live events, such as product launches or conferences, by providing attendees with interactive, virtual experiences that complement the physical event.

3. Preparing for the Future of AR and VR in Marketing:

- Stay informed: Keep up with the latest developments in AR and VR technologies and their applications in marketing, ensuring that you are aware of emerging trends and best practices.

- Invest in skills development: Encourage your marketing team to develop skills in AR and VR, such as content creation, 3D modeling, and user experience design.

- Experiment with AR and VR platforms: Test and evaluate different AR and VR marketing tools and platforms to determine which ones best meet your needs and can help you achieve your marketing objectives.

- Collaborate with experts: Partner with AR and VR experts or consultancies to leverage their knowledge and expertise in implementing these technologies in your marketing efforts.

In conclusion, the impact of AR and VR on marketing is set to revolutionize the industry, offering new opportunities for enhanced customer experiences, improved product visualization, increased brand awareness, and personalized experiences. By staying informed about these emerging technologies, investing in skills development, experimenting with AR and VR platforms, and collaborating with experts, marketers can effectively harness the power of AR and VR to enhance their marketing strategies and drive future success.

Part 3: The Rise of Voice and Conversational Marketing

The increasing popularity of voice assistants and smart speakers has led to a significant shift in the way people interact with technology. Voice and conversational marketing are emerging as essential components of modern marketing strategies, as brands strive to create more natural and engaging experiences for their customers. In this part, we will discuss the rise of voice and conversational marketing and explore some of the ways these trends are shaping the future of the industry.

1. The Impact of Voice and Conversational Marketing on Marketing:

- Improved customer engagement: Voice and conversational marketing enable brands to connect with their customers through more natural and intuitive interactions, resulting in higher levels of engagement.

- Enhanced personalization: By leveraging data from voice interactions, marketers can gain valuable insights into individual customer preferences and tailor their marketing efforts accordingly.

- Expanded reach: Voice marketing allows brands to reach new audiences, such as users with visual impairments or those who prefer hands-free interactions.

- Increased efficiency: Conversational marketing can streamline the customer journey by providing quick and easy access to information and support through voice-based interactions.

2. Examples of Voice and Conversational Marketing Applications:

- Voice-activated content: Brands can create voice-activated content, such as podcasts, news briefings, or guided meditations, that can be accessed through voice assistants and smart speakers.

- Voice search optimization: As voice search becomes more

prevalent, marketers must optimize their content and website structure to be easily discoverable through voice-based queries.

- Voice-based advertising: Brands can leverage voice ads on platforms such as Amazon Alexa or Google Assistant to reach customers through audio content and voice-enabled devices.

- Chatbots and virtual assistants: Conversational AI-powered chatbots can provide personalized support and assistance through voice or text-based interactions, guiding customers through the purchasing process and answering frequently asked questions.

3. Preparing for the Future of Voice and Conversational Marketing:

- Stay informed: Keep up with the latest developments in voice and conversational marketing technologies and their applications in marketing, ensuring that you are aware of emerging trends and best practices.

- Invest in skills development: Encourage your marketing team to develop skills in voice and conversational marketing, such as voice user interface design, conversational copywriting, and voice search optimization.

- Experiment with voice-based platforms: Test and evaluate different voice and conversational marketing tools and platforms to determine which ones best meet your needs and can help you achieve your marketing objectives.

- Collaborate with experts: Partner with voice and conversational marketing experts or consultancies to leverage their knowledge and expertise in implementing these technologies in your marketing efforts.

In conclusion, the rise of voice and conversational marketing is set to transform the industry, offering new opportunities for improved customer engagement, enhanced personalization, expanded reach, and increased efficiency. By staying informed about these emerging trends, investing in skills development, experimenting with voice-based platforms, and collaborating with experts, marketers can effectively harness the power of voice and conversational marketing to enhance their marketing strategies and drive future success.

Part 4: Preparing for the Future of Marketing and Beyond

As the marketing landscape continues to evolve, it is crucial for marketers to stay ahead of emerging trends and technologies to ensure their strategies remain relevant and effective. This final part of the chapter will provide insights on how to prepare for the future of marketing and beyond, including tips on staying informed, fostering a culture of innovation, and embracing change.

1. Stay informed and proactive:

   - Monitor industry news: Keep up with the latest developments in marketing, technology, and consumer behavior to stay informed about emerging trends and best practices.

   - Participate in industry events: Attend conferences, workshops, and webinars to gain insights from thought leaders, learn about new technologies, and network with peers.

   - Invest in ongoing education: Encourage your marketing team to pursue professional development opportunities, such as online courses, certifications, or workshops, to stay current with the latest marketing tools and techniques.

2. Foster a culture of innovation and experimentation:

   - Encourage creativity: Create an environment that supports and celebrates creative thinking, and encourage your team to explore new ideas and approaches.

   - Embrace failure: Recognize that not all experiments will be successful, and view failures as valuable learning opportunities that can inform future strategies.

   - Implement agile methodologies: Adopt agile marketing practices, such as iterative planning and data-driven decision-making, to enable your team to adapt quickly to changing market conditions and consumer preferences.

3. Embrace new technologies and platforms:

- Evaluate emerging tools: Regularly assess the latest marketing tools and platforms to determine which ones have the potential to enhance your marketing efforts and help you achieve your objectives.

- Invest in technology: Allocate resources to invest in new technologies that can streamline your marketing processes, improve customer experiences, and drive growth.

- Partner with experts: Collaborate with technology experts or consultancies to leverage their knowledge and expertise in implementing new tools and platforms in your marketing efforts.

4. Focus on customer-centricity:

- Put the customer first: Ensure that your marketing strategies prioritize the needs, preferences, and expectations of your customers, fostering long-term loyalty and advocacy.

- Embrace personalization: Leverage data and insights to create personalized marketing experiences that cater to individual customer preferences and behaviors.

- Continuously optimize the customer journey: Regularly assess and refine your customer touchpoints to ensure a seamless, enjoyable experience across all channels and stages of the buyer's journey.

5. Prepare for ethical and sustainable marketing practices:

- Commit to ethical marketing: Develop and adhere to a code of ethics that outlines your organization's commitment to responsible, honest, and transparent marketing practices.

- Prioritize sustainability: Incorporate sustainable practices into your marketing efforts, such as reducing waste, embracing eco-friendly materials, and supporting social causes.

- Build trust and authenticity: Foster long-lasting customer relationships by being transparent, authentic, and accountable in all of your marketing initiatives.

In conclusion, preparing for the future of marketing and beyond requires staying informed, fostering a culture of innovation, embracing new technologies, focusing on customer-centricity, and committing to ethical and sustainable practices. By adopting these strategies, marketers can effectively navigate the ever-changing marketing landscape and drive ongoing success for their brands.

In conclusion, "The Art of Marketing: Mastering Strategies for Success in a Dynamic Landscape" has provided a comprehensive exploration of the multifaceted world of marketing, delving into key principles, strategies, tools, and future trends that are shaping the industry. By examining these diverse aspects of marketing, this book has aimed to equip readers with the knowledge, insights, and best practices needed to excel in this rapidly evolving field.

Throughout the book, we have explored the fundamental building blocks of marketing, from understanding the marketing mix, market segmentation, and targeting, to positioning and differentiation, and building a strong brand identity. We have also examined the essential role of consumer behavior in marketing, discussing the factors that influence consumer choices and how marketers can leverage these insights to create more effective campaigns.

In addition, the book has delved into the importance of crafting compelling marketing strategies and using storytelling as a powerful tool for connecting with audiences. The chapters on digital marketing mastery and data-driven marketing decisions have highlighted the critical role that technology plays in modern marketing, discussing the various tools and techniques available to marketers for reaching and engaging customers in the digital age.

Moreover, we have covered the art of creating successful marketing campaigns and the importance of building long-term customer relationships through CRM strategies, personalization, and loyalty programs. The book has also addressed the significance of ethical marketing practices, emphasizing the need for marketers to prioritize transparency, authenticity, and social responsibility in their efforts.

Lastly, we have discussed the future trends in marketing, including the growing role of artificial intelligence, augmented and virtual reality, voice and conversational marketing, and the importance of preparing for these emerging technologies and practices. By staying informed, fostering a culture of innovation, embracing new technologies, focusing on customer-centricity, and committing to ethical and sustainable practices, marketers can successfully navigate the ever-changing marketing landscape and drive ongoing success for their brands.

In a world where marketing is constantly evolving, this book serves as a valuable resource for both new and experienced marketers, providing a comprehensive guide to navigating the complexities of the industry. By mastering the strategies, tools, and techniques outlined in this book, readers will be well-prepared to face the challenges and seize the opportunities presented by the dynamic world of marketing, ultimately empowering them to create meaningful, impactful, and successful marketing campaigns that resonate with their target audiences and drive business growth.

We hope that "The Art of Marketing" has inspired and empowered you to embrace the endless possibilities that marketing has to offer, and we encourage you to use the knowledge and insights gained from this book to continually refine your marketing skills, push the boundaries of innovation, and contribute to shaping the future of this exciting and ever-evolving industry.

NOTES:

NOTES:

NOTES:

NOTES:

NOTES:

NOTES:

www.ingramcontent.com/pod-product-compliance
Lightning Source LLC
Chambersburg PA
CBHW070655220526
45466CB00001B/445